The Truth About Angels

*A behind-the-scenes view
of supernatural beings involved
in human life*

Ellen G. White

 **Pacific Press®**
Publishing Association

Nampa, Idaho
www.pacificpress.com

Cover Illustration by Lee Christiansen

Copyright © 1996 by
Pacific Press® Publishing Association
Printed in United States of America
All Rights Reserved
Typeset in 10/12 Century Schoolbook

To convey the nineteenth-century intent of the author,
in this volume the occurrences of the word
"intercourse" have been replaced by "interaction." The
word "gay" has been replaced by "pleasure-seeking."

**Library of Congress Cataloging-in-Publication
Data:**

White, Ellen Gould Harmon, 1827-1915.
    The Truth About Angels : a behind-the-scenes view
    of supernatural beings involved in human life / Ellen
    Gould White
        p.   cm.
    ISBN 978-0-8163-2038-7
    1. Angels. 2. Seventh-Day Adventist—Doctrines.
I. White, Ellen Gould, 1827-1915. II. Title.
BT966.W47 1996   95-46980
235'.3—dc20   CIP

October 2019

Abbreviations
of Sources

AA	*The Acts of the Apostles*
AUCR	*Australian Union Conference Recorder*
AUG	*Atlantic Union Gleaner*
AY	*Appeal to Youth*
BE	*Bible Echo*
BE&ST	*Bible Echo and Signs of the Times*
CC	*Conflict and Courage*
CH	*Counsels on Health*
CG	*Child Guidance*
COL	*Christ's Object Lessons*
CW	*Counsels to Writers and Editors*
DA	*The Desire of Ages*
Ed	*Education*
FCE	*Fundamentals of Christian Education*
GC	*The Great Controversy Between Christ and Satan*
GCB	*General Conference Bulletin*
GW	*Gospel Workers*
HL	*Healthful Living*
HP	*In Heavenly Places*
HR	*The Health Reformer*
HS	*Historical Sketches of SDA Foreign Missions*
LDE	*Last Day Events*
LP	*Sketches From the Life of Paul*
LS	*Life Sketches*
Mar	*Maranatha*
ML	*My Life Today*

To the Reader

This book deals with a subject of worldwide interest. In unprecedented numbers, television programs feature purported accounts of angel involvement in human affairs. Tabloid newspapers publish stories about numerous reported sightings of extraterrestrial visitors. Bookstores display shelf after shelf of volumes dealing with the supernatural, and sales are brisk. In every land people are asking questions such as, If angels actually exist, who are they? Are they the spirits of the dead? Are they friendly or hostile? Can they communicate with us?

Most answers given by "authorities" do not satisfy the sincere seeker for truth. Many of the answers represent mere speculation. Some are purposely sensational. Others are based on false interpretations of Scripture.

By contrast, the present volume is filled with inspired information. It offers answers grounded firmly in the Word of God. It not only sets forth the truth about angels, but, we believe, will lead the reader into a deeper spiritual experience.

The first chapter provides a general overview of the existence and activities of beings in the unseen world. The second chapter illustrates a few of the numerous ways in which angels are involved in the personal lives of human beings. Beginning with chapter 3, the book sets forth in historical sequence a galaxy of events and experiences in which angels have been major players.

It begins with the rebellion of Lucifer in heaven before the creation of this world and concludes with the role of angels in the great hereafter.

This volume is a priceless resource book, but it is much more than that; it is a book that lifts the veil between the seen and the unseen world. It reveals angel involvement in events that secular historians recorded but could not explain, and gives the reader the feeling that he or she is an eyewitness of these events—an exciting experience indeed!

We believe that this book will be prized by seekers of truth all over the world, that it will help them recognize counterfeit manifestations of spirits, and that in their daily walk with God it will lead them to seek and enjoy the fellowship of holy angels.

Contents

1.

Angels and You— a Brief Overview

The connection of the visible with the invisible world, the ministration of angels of God, and the agency of evil spirits, are plainly revealed in the Scriptures, and inseparably interwoven with human history. . . .

Before the creation of man, angels were in existence; for when the foundations of the earth were laid, "the morning stars sang together, and all the sons of God shouted for joy." Job 38:7. . . . Angels are in nature superior to men, for the psalmist says that man was made "a little lower than the angels." Psalm 8:5.

The Number and Power of Angels

We are informed in Scripture as to the number, and the power and glory, of the heavenly beings, of their connection with the government of God, and also of their relation to the work of redemption. "The Lord hath prepared His throne in the heavens; and His kingdom ruleth over all." And, says the prophet, "I heard the voice of many angels round about the throne." In the presence chamber of the King of kings they wait—"angels, that excel in strength," "ministers of His, that do His pleasure," "hearkening unto the voice of His word." Psalm 103:19-21; Revelation 5:11.

Ten thousand times ten thousand and thousands of thousands, were the heavenly messengers beheld by the prophet Daniel. The apostle Paul declared them "an innumerable company." Daniel 7:10; Hebrews 12:22. As God's messengers they go forth, like "the appearance of a flash of lightning," (Ezekiel 1:14), so dazzling their glory, and so swift their flight. The angel that appeared at the Saviour's tomb, his countenance "like lightning, and his raiment white as snow," caused the keepers for fear of him to quake, and they "became as dead men." Matthew 28:3, 4.

When Sennacherib, the haughty Assyrian, reproached and blasphemed God, and threatened Israel with destruction, "it came to pass that night, that the angel of the Lord went out, and smote in the camp of the Assyrians an hundred fourscore and five thousand." There were "cut off all the mighty men of valor, and the leaders and captains," from the army of Sennacherib. "So he returned with shame of face to his own land." 2 Kings 19:35; 2 Chronicles 32:21.

Angels Help God's Children

Angels are sent on missions of mercy to the children of God. To Abraham, with promises of blessing; to the gates of Sodom, to rescue righteous Lot from its fiery doom; to Elijah, as he was about to perish from weariness and hunger in the desert; to Elisha, with chariots and horses of fire surrounding the little town where he was shut in by his foes; to Daniel, while seeking divine wisdom in the court of a heathen king, or abandoned to become the lions' prey; to Peter, doomed to death in Herod's dungeon; to the prisoners at Philippi; to Paul and His companions in the night of tempest on the sea; to open the mind of Cornelius to receive the gospel; to dispatch Peter with the message of salvation to the Gentile stranger—thus holy angels have, in all ages, ministered to God's people.

Thus God's people, exposed to the deceptive power and unsleeping malice of the prince of darkness, and in conflict with all the forces of evil, are assured of the unceasing guardianship of heavenly angels. Nor is such assurance given without need. If God has granted to His children promise of grace and protection, it is because there are mighty agencies of evil to be met—agencies numerous, determined, and untiring, of whose malignity and power none can safely be ignorant or unheeding.

Satan and Evil Angels

Evil spirits, in the beginning created sinless, were equal in nature, power, and glory with the holy beings that are now God's messengers. But fallen through sin, they are leagued together for the dishonor of God and the destruction of men. United with Satan in his rebellion, and with him cast out from heaven, they have, through all succeeding ages, cooperated with him in his warfare against the divine authority. We are told in Scripture of their confederacy and government, of their various orders, of their intelligence and subtlety, and of their malicious designs against the peace and happiness of men. . . .

None are in greater danger from the influence of evil spirits than those who, notwithstanding the direct and ample testimony of the Scriptures, deny the existence and agency of the devil and his angels. So long as we are ignorant of their wiles, they have almost inconceivable advantage; many give heed to their suggestions while they suppose themselves to be following the dictates of their own wisdom. This is why, as we approach the close of time, when Satan is to work with greatest power to deceive and destroy, he spreads everywhere the belief that he does not exist. It is his policy to conceal himself and his manner of working. . . .

It is because he has masked himself with consummate skill that the question is so widely asked: "Does such a being really exist?" It is an evidence of his success that theories giving the lie to the plainest testimony of the Scriptures are so generally received in the religious world. And it is because Satan can most readily control the minds of those who are unconscious of his influence, that the Word of God gives us so many examples of his malignant work, unveiling before us his secret forces, and thus placing us on our guard against his assaults.

Christ's Followers Are Safe

The power and malice of Satan and his host might justly alarm us were it not that we may find shelter and deliverance in the superior power of our Redeemer. We carefully secure our houses with bolts and locks to protect our property and our lives from evil men; but we seldom think of the evil angels who are constantly seeking access to us, and against whose attacks we have, in our own strength, no method of defense. If permitted, they can distract our minds, disorder and torment our bodies, destroy our possessions and our lives. Their only delight is in misery and destruction.

Fearful is the condition of those who resist the divine claims and yield to Satan's temptations, until God gives them up to the control of evil spirits. But those who follow Christ are ever safe under His watchcare. Angels that excel in strength are sent from heaven to protect them. The wicked one cannot break through the guard which God has stationed about His people. —GC 511-513, 516, 517.

2.

Angel Ministry Today

Angels Guard Us

A guardian angel is appointed to every follower of Christ. These heavenly watchers shield the righteous from the power of the wicked one. This Satan himself recognized when he said: "Doth Job fear God for nought? Hast not Thou made an hedge about him, and about his house, and about all that he hath on every side?" Job 1: 9, 10. The agency by which God protects His people is presented in the words of the psalmist: "The angel of the Lord encampeth round about them that fear Him, and delivereth them." Psalm 34:7. Said the Saviour, speaking of those that believe in Him: "Take heed that ye despise not one of these little ones; for I say unto you, That in heaven their angels do always behold the face of My Father." Matthew 18:10. The angels appointed to minister to the children of God have at all times access to His presence.—GC 512, 513.

We know not what results a day, an hour, or a moment may determine, and never should we begin the day without committing our ways to our heavenly Father. His angels are appointed to watch over us, and if we put ourselves under their guardianship, then in every time of danger they will be at our right hand. When unconsciously we are in danger of exerting a wrong influence, the angels will be by our side, prompting us to a better course, choosing our words for us, and influencing our actions.—COL 341, 342.

Angels of God are all around us. . . . Oh, we want to know these things, and fear and tremble, and to think much more of the power of the angels of God that are watching over and guarding us than we have done hitherto. . . . Angels of God are commissioned from heaven to guard the children of men, and yet they draw away from their restraining influences and go where they can have communication with the evil angels. . . . Oh, that we might all obey the injunction of the apostle (read 2 Corinthians 6:17, 18).—5MR 125.

Angels are sent to minister to the children of God who are physically blind. Angels guard their steps and save them from a thousand dangers, which, unknown to them, beset their path.—WM 240.

I was today to write upon Christ walking on the sea and stilling the tempest. Oh, how this scene was impressed upon my mind. . . . The majesty of God and His works occupied my thoughts. He holds the winds in His hands, He controls the waters. Finite beings, mere specks upon the broad, deep waters of the Pacific, were we in the sight of God, yet angels of heaven were sent from His excellent glory to guard that little sailboat that was careening over the waves.—TDG 110.

Angels Involved in Family Life

The Lord is served as much, yes, more, by the faithful home worker as by the one who preaches the Word. Fathers and mothers should realize that they are the educators of their children. Children are the heritage of the Lord; and they should be trained and disciplined to form characters that the Lord can approve. When this work is carried on judiciously and with faithfulness and prayer, angels of God will guard the family, and the most commonplace life will be made sacred. —AUCR Sept. 6, 1909.

Before leaving the house for labor, all the family should be called together; and the father, or the mother in the father's absence, should plead fervently with God to keep them through the day. Come in humility, with a heart full of tenderness, and with a sense of the temptations and dangers before yourselves and your children; by faith bind them upon the altar, entreating for them the care of the Lord. Ministering angels will guard children who are thus dedicated to God.—CG 519.

The angels of God, thousands upon thousands, . . . guard us against evil and press back the powers of darkness that are seeking our destruction. Have we not reason to be thankful every moment, thankful even when there are apparent difficulties in our pathway?—ML 171.

Angels of God are watching over us. Upon this earth there are thousands and tens of thousands of heavenly messengers commissioned by the Father to prevent

Satan from obtaining any advantage over those who refuse to walk in the path of evil. And these angels who guard God's children on earth are in communication with the Father in heaven.—HP 99.

We need to understand better than we do the mission of the angels. It would be well to remember that every true child of God has the cooperation of heavenly beings. Invisible armies of light and power attend the meek and lowly ones who believe and claim the promises of God. Cherubim and seraphim, and angels that excel in strength, stand at God's right hand, "All ministering spirits, sent forth to minister for them who shall be heirs of salvation."—AA 154.

Angels Enlighten Our Minds

God calls upon His creatures to turn their attention from the confusion and perplexity around them and admire His handiwork. The heavenly bodies are worthy of contemplation. God has made them for the benefit of man, and as we study His works, angels of God will be by our side to enlighten our minds and guard them from satanic deception.—4BC 1145.

Heavenly angels watch those who are seeking for enlightenment. They cooperate with those who try to win souls to Christ.—BE&ST Dec. 10, 1900.

Your . . . [ministry to] the sick is an exhausting process and would gradually dry up the very springs of life if there were no change, no opportunity for recreation, and if angels of God did not guard and protect you. If you could see the many perils through which you are conducted safely every day by these messengers of heaven, gratitude would spring up in your hearts and find expression from your lips. If you make God your strength, you may, under the most discouraging circumstances, attain a height and breadth of Christian perfection which you hardly think it possible to reach. Your thoughts may be elevated, you may have noble aspirations, clear perceptions of truth, and purposes of action which shall raise you above all sordid motives.—CH 384.

I have been shown your [a physician's] peril, and I have also been shown your guardian angel preserving you again and again from yourself, keeping you from making shipwreck of faith. My brother, lift up the standard, lift it up, and be not fainthearted or discouraged. —8T 175.

Angels Help Us Do Right

Learn to trust in God. Learn to go to Him who is mighty to save. . . . Tell the dear Saviour just what you need. He that said, "Suffer little children to come unto me, and forbid them not," will not reject your prayer. But He will send His angels to guard you and protect you from the evil angels, and will make it easy for you to do right. Then it will be much easier than if you should try in your own strength. You may ever feel like this: "I have asked God to help me, and He will do it. I will do right in His strength. I will not grieve the dear angels that God has appointed to watch over me. I will never take a course to drive them from me."—AY 55, 56.

If you will try to suppress every evil thought through the day, then the angels of God will come and dwell with you. These angels are beings that excel in strength. You remember how the angel came to the sepulcher, and the Roman soldiers fell like dead men before the glory of his countenance; and if one angel could work with such power, how would it have been if all the angels that are with us here, had been present? The angels are with us every day, to guard and protect us from the assaults of the enemy.

You are not alone in the warfare against wrong. Could the curtain be rolled back, you would see heavenly angels fighting with you. This they must do; it is their work to guard the youth. "Are they not all ministering spirits, sent forth to minister for them who shall be heirs of salvation?" Ten thousand times ten thousand and thousands of thousands of angels minister to the youth.—YI Jan. 1, 1903.

I am very thankful that I could visit your school [now Oakwood College]. For years I have done what I could to help the colored people, and I have never found the work so well begun in any place as I find it here at the present time. In all your experiences, remember that angels of God are beside you. They know what you do; they are present to guard you. Do not do anything to displease them. As you work and they work, this school will become consecrated ground. I shall want to hear how you succeed. All heaven is interested in the moves you are making. Let us do our utmost to help one another to obtain the victory. Let us so live that the light of heaven can shine into our hearts and minds, enabling us to grasp the treasures of heaven. —SF Echo June 1, 1909.

Angels Aid Efforts for the Lost

When heavenly intelligences see those who claim to be sons and daughters of God putting forth Christlike efforts to help the erring, manifesting a tender, sympathetic spirit for the repentant and the fallen, angels press close to them, and bring to their remembrance the very words that will soothe and uplift the soul. . . . Jesus has given His precious life, His personal attention, to the least of God's little ones; and the angels that excel in strength encamp round about them that fear God.—HL 277.

Angels are sent from the heavenly courts, not to destroy, but to watch over and guard imperiled souls, to save the lost, to bring the straying ones back to the fold. "I came not to condemn, but to save," Christ declared. Have you, then, no pitying words to speak to the straying? Will you let them perish, or will you reach out to them a helping hand? Right around you there are souls who are in danger of perishing. Will you not with the cords of love draw them to the Saviour? Will you not cease your reproaches, and speak words that will inspire them with faith and courage?—RH May 10, 1906.

It is the privilege of all who comply with the conditions to know for themselves that pardon is freely extended for every sin. Put away the suspicion that God's promises are not meant for you. They are for every repentant transgressor. Strength and grace have been provided through Christ to be brought by ministering angels to every believing soul.—SC 52.

Those who labor for the good of others are working in union with the heavenly angels. They have their constant companionship, their unceasing ministry. Angels of light and power are ever near, to protect, to comfort, to heal, to instruct, to inspire. The highest education, the truest culture, the most exalted service possible to human beings in this world, are theirs. —RH July 11, 1912.

The angels of heaven are moving upon human minds to arouse investigation in the themes of the Bible. A far greater work will be done than has yet been done and none of the glory of it will flow to men, for angels that minister to those who shall be heirs of salvation are working night and day.—CW 140.

God might have committed the message of the gospel, and all the work of loving ministry, to the heavenly angels. He might have employed other means for accomplishing His purpose. But in His infinite love He chose to make us co-workers with Himself, with Christ and the angels, that we might share the blessing, the joy, the spiritual uplifting, which results from this unselfish ministry.—SC 79.

Angels Strengthen Our Faith

"The angel of the Lord encampeth round about them that fear Him, and delivereth them." Psalm 34:7. God commissions His angels to save His chosen ones from calamity, to guard them from "the pestilence that walketh in darkness" and "the destruction that wasteth at noonday." Psalm 91:6. Again and again have angels talked with men as a man speaketh with a friend, and led them to places of security. Again and again have the encouraging words of angels renewed the drooping spirits of the faithful and, carrying their minds above the things of earth, caused them to behold by faith the white robes, the crowns, the palm branches of victory, which overcomers will receive when they surround the great white throne.—AA 153.

"Among these that stand by"—the hosts of the enemy, who are trying to bring God's people into disrepute, and the hosts of heaven, ten thousand times ten thousand angels, who watch over and guard the tempted people of God, uplifting and strengthening them. These are they who stand by. And God says to His believing ones, You shall walk among them. You shall not be overcome by the powers of darkness. You shall stand before Me in the sight of the holy angels, who are sent forth to minister to those who shall be heirs of salvation.—GCB April 2, 1901.

3.

Angels in Heaven, Before the Rebellion

Christ as Creator-God

Before men or angels were created, the Word was with God, and was God.

The world was made by Him, "and without Him was not anything made that was made." If Christ made all things, He existed before all things. The words spoken in regard to this are so decisive that no one need be left in doubt. Christ was God essentially, and in the highest sense. He was with God from all eternity, God over all, blessed forevermore.

The Lord Jesus Christ, the divine Son of God, existed from eternity, a distinct person, yet one with the Father. He was the surpassing glory of heaven. He was the commander of the heavenly intelligences, and the adoring homage of the angels was received by Him as His right.—RH April 5, 1906.

Through Solomon Christ declared: "The Lord possessed Me in the beginning of His way, before His works of old. I was set up from everlasting, from the beginning, or ever the earth was. . . . When He gave to the sea His decree, that the waters should not pass His commandment; when He appointed the foundations of the earth; then I was by Him, as one brought up with Him; and I was daily His delight, rejoicing always before Him." [Prov. 8:22-25, 29, 30.]

In speaking of His pre-existence, Christ carries the mind back through dateless ages. He assures us that there never was a time when He was not in close fellowship with the eternal God. He . . . had been with God as one brought up with Him.—ST Aug. 29, 1900.

What is the work of angels in comparison with His [Christ's] condescension? His throne is from everlasting. He has reared every arch and pillar in nature's great temple.—HP 40.

Christ the Word, the Only Begotten of God, was one with the eternal Father—one in nature, in character, and in purpose—the only being in all the universe that could enter into all the counsels and purposes of God. —GC 493.

Before Sin Arose, God Had a Plan

God and Christ knew from the beginning of the apostasy of Satan and of the fall of Adam through the deceptive power of the apostate. The plan of salvation was designed to redeem the fallen race, to give them another trial. Christ was appointed to the office of Mediator from the creation of God, set up from everlasting to be our substitute and surety.—1SM 250.

Known unto God are all His works, and from eternal ages the covenant of grace (unmerited favor) existed in the mind of God. It is called the everlasting covenant; for the plan of salvation was not conceived after the fall of man, but it was that which was "kept in silence through times eternal, but now is manifested, and by the Scriptures of the prophets, according to the commandment of the eternal God, is made known unto all the nations unto obedience of faith." Rom. 16:25, 26, A.R.V.—ST Dec. 5, 1914.

The plan for our redemption was not an afterthought, a plan formulated after the fall of Adam. It was a revelation of "the mystery which hath been kept in silence through times eternal." Rom. 16:25, R.V. It was an unfolding of the principles that from eternal ages have been the foundation of God's throne. . . . God did not ordain that sin should exist, but He foresaw its existence, and made provision to meet the terrible emergency.—DA 22.

Creation of the Angels

The Father wrought by His Son in the creation of all heavenly beings. "By Him were all things created, . . . whether they be thrones, or dominions, or principalities, or powers; all things were created by Him, and for Him."—PP 34.

Before the creation of man, angels were in existence; for when the foundations of the earth were laid, "the morning stars sang together, and all the sons of God shouted for joy." Job 38:7. After the fall of man, angels were sent to guard the tree of life, and this before a human being had died. Angels are in nature superior to men, for the psalmist says that man was made "a little lower than the angels." Psalm 8:5.—GC 511.

From eternal ages it was God's purpose that every created being, from the bright and holy seraph to man, should be a temple for the indwelling of the Creator. —DA 161.

All created beings live by the will and power of God. They are dependent recipients of the life of God. From the highest seraph to the humblest animate being, all are replenished from the Source of life.—DA 785.

When the Lord created these [angelic] beings to stand before His throne, they were beautiful and glorious. Their loveliness and holiness were equal to their exalted station. They were enriched by the wisdom of God, and girded with the panoply of heaven.—ST April 14, 1898.

Creation of Lucifer

God made him [Lucifer] good and beautiful, as near as possible like Himself.—RH Sept. 24, 1901.

God had made him [Lucifer] noble, had given him rich endowments. He gave him a high, responsible position. He asked of him nothing that was unreasonable.

He was to administer the trust given him of God in a spirit of meekness and devotion, seeking to promote the glory of God, who had given him glory and beauty and loveliness.—SSW March 1, 1893.

Though God had created Lucifer noble and beautiful, and had exalted him to high honor among the angelic host, yet he had not placed him beyond the possibility of evil. It was in Satan's* power, did he choose to do so, to pervert these gifts.—4SP 317.

Lucifer's High Position

Lucifer in heaven, before his rebellion, was a high and exalted angel, next in honor to God's dear Son. His countenance, like those of the other angels, was mild and expressive of happiness. His forehead was high and broad, showing a powerful intellect. His form was perfect; his bearing noble and majestic. A special light beamed in his countenance and shone around him brighter and more beautiful than around the other angels; yet Christ, God's dear Son, had the pre-eminence over all the angelic host. He was one with the Father before the angels were created.—SR 13.

Lucifer was the covering cherub, the most exalted of the heavenly created beings; he stood nearest the

---

* Ellen White sometimes used prolepsis—i.e., speaking of something in the future as if it had already happened. Here she referred to Lucifer as "Satan" even though he had not yet rebelled. Since she used the two names—Lucifer and Satan—without making a distinction between them, this compilation has followed her usage.

throne of God, and was most closely connected and identified with the administration of God's government,
most richly endowed with the glory of His majesty and
power.—ST April 28, 1890.

The Lord Himself gave to Satan his glory and wisdom, and made him the covering cherub, good, noble,
and exceeding lovely.—ST Sept. 18, 1893.

Among the inhabitants of heaven, Satan, next to
Christ, was at one time most honored of God, and highest in power and glory.—ST July 23, 1902.

Lucifer, the "son of the morning," in glory surpassing all the angels that surround the throne, . . . [was]
united in closest ties to the Son of God.—DA 435.

Lucifer, "son of the morning," was first of the covering cherubs, holy and undefiled. He stood in the presence of the great Creator, and the ceaseless beams of
glory enshrouding the eternal God rested upon him.
—PP 35.

He [Lucifer] had been the highest of all created beings, and had been foremost in revealing God's purposes to the universe.—DA 758.

Before Evil Originated

Peace and joy, in perfect submission to the will of
Heaven, existed throughout the angelic host. Love
to God was supreme, love for one another impartial.

Such was the condition that existed for ages before the entrance of sin.—4SP 316, 317.

He [Lucifer] had a knowledge of the inestimable value of eternal riches that man did not possess. He had experienced the pure contentment, the peace, the exalted happiness and unalloyed joys, of the heavenly abode. He had realized, before his rebellion, the satisfaction of the full approval of God. He had had a full appreciation of the glory that enshrouded the Father, and knew that there was no limit to His power.—ST Aug. 4, 1887.

There was a time when . . . it was his [Satan's] joy to execute the divine commands. His heart was filled with love and joy in serving his Creator.—ST Sept. 18, 1893.

Satan was a beautiful, exalted angel, and would have remained so forever had he not withdrawn his allegiance from God.—ST Dec. 21, 1891.

4.

The Origin of Evil

The Origin of Evil a Mystery

The angels had been created full of goodness and love. They loved one another impartially and their God supremely, and they were prompted by this love to do His pleasure. The law of God was not a grievous yoke to them, but it was their delight to do His commandments, to hearken unto the voice of His Word. But in this state of peace and purity, sin originated with him who had been perfect in all his ways. The prophet writes of him: "Thine heart was lifted up because of thy beauty; thou hast corrupted thy wisdom by reason of thy brightness." Sin is a mysterious, unexplainable thing. There was no reason for its existence; to seek to explain it is to seek to give a reason for it, and that would be to justify it. Sin appeared in a perfect universe, a thing that was shown to be inexcusable.—ST April 28, 1890.

God had a knowledge of the events of the future, even before the creation of the world. He did not make His purposes to fit circumstances, but He allowed matters to develop and work out. He did not work to bring about a certain condition of things, but He knew that such a condition would exist. The plan that should be carried out upon the defection of any of the high intelligences of heaven—this is the secret, the mystery which has been hid from ages. And an offering was prepared in the eternal purposes to do the very work which God has done for fallen humanity.—ST March 25, 1897.

The entrance of sin into heaven cannot be explained. If it were explainable, it would show that there was some reason for sin. But as there was not the least excuse for it, its origin will ever remain shrouded in mystery.—RH March 9, 1886.

God did not create evil. He only made the good, which was like Himself. . . . Evil, sin, and death . . . are the result of disobedience, which originated in Satan. —RH Aug. 4, 1910.

The First Inklings of Evil

There was a time when Satan was in harmony with God, and it was his joy to execute the divine commands. His heart was filled with love and joy in serving his Creator, until he began to think that his wisdom was not derived from God, but was inherent in himself, and that he was as worthy as was God to receive honor and power.—ST Sept. 18, 1893.

Though God had created Lucifer noble and beautiful, and had exalted him to high honor among the angelic host, yet He had not placed him beyond the possibility of evil. It was in Satan's power, did he choose to do so, to pervert these gifts. He might have remained in favor with God, beloved and honored by all the angelic throng, presiding in his exalted position with generous, unselfish care, exercising his noble powers to bless others and to glorify his Maker. But, little by little, he began to seek his own honor, and to employ his powers to attract attention and win praise to himself. He also gradually led the angels, over whom he ruled, to do him service instead of devoting all their powers to the service of their Creator.—4SP 317.

Little by little, Lucifer came to indulge the desire for self-exaltation. . . . Though all his glory was from God, this mighty angel came to regard it as pertaining to himself.—PP 35.

God Sets Forth Christ's True Position

Before the great contest should open, all were to have a clear presentation of His [God's] will, whose wisdom and goodness were the spring of all their joy.

The King of the universe summoned the heavenly host before Him, that in their presence He might set forth the true position of His Son, and show the relation He sustained to all created beings. . . . Before the assembled inhabitants of heaven the King declared that none but Christ, the Only Begotten of God, could fully enter into His purposes, and to Him it was committed to execute the mighty counsels of His will.—PP 36.

The great Creator assembled the heavenly host, that He might in the presence of all the angels confer special honor upon His Son. The Son was seated on the throne with the Father, and the heavenly throng of holy angels was gathered around them. The Father then made known that it was ordained by Himself that Christ, His Son, should be equal with Himself; so that wherever was the presence of His Son, it was as His own presence. The word of the Son was to be obeyed as readily as the word of the Father. His Son He had invested with authority to command the heavenly host. Especially was His Son to work in union with Himself in the anticipated creation of the earth. . . .

Satan was envious and jealous of Jesus Christ. Yet when all the angels bowed to Jesus to acknowledge His supremacy and high authority and rightful rule, Satan bowed with them; but his heart was filled with envy and hatred. Christ had been taken into the special counsel of God in regard to His plans, while Satan was unacquainted with them. He did not understand, neither was he permitted to know, the purposes of God. But Christ was acknowledged sovereign of heaven, His power and authority to be the same as that of God Himself.

Satan thought that he was himself a favorite in heaven among the angels. He had been highly exalted; but . . . he aspired to the height of God Himself. He gloried in his loftiness. He knew that he was honored by the angels. He had a special mission to execute. He had been near the great Creator, and the ceaseless beams of glorious light enshrouding the eternal God, had shone especially upon him. Satan thought how angels had obeyed his command with pleasurable alacrity. Were not his garments light and

beautiful? Why should Christ thus be honored before himself?—1SP 17, 18.

The angels joyfully acknowledged the supremacy of
Christ, and prostrating themselves before Him, poured
out their love and adoration. Lucifer bowed with them,
but in his heart there was a strange, fierce conflict.
Truth, justice, and loyalty were struggling against envy
and jealousy. The influence of the holy angels seemed
for a time to carry him with them. . . . But again he
was filled with pride in his own glory. His desire for
supremacy returned, and envy of Christ was once more
indulged.—PP 36, 37.

Lucifer Begins His Campaign Against Christ

Satan . . . began his work of rebellion with the angels under his command, seeking to diffuse among them
the spirit of discontent. And he worked in so deceptive
a way that many of the angels were won to his allegiance before his purposes were fully known.—RH Jan.
28, 1909.

Satan . . . had been ambitious for the more exalted
honors which God had bestowed upon His Son. He became envious of Christ, and represented to the angels
who honored him as covering cherub that he had not
the honor conferred upon him which his position demanded.—RH Feb. 24, 1874.

By sly insinuations, by which he made it appear
that Christ had assumed the place that belonged to

himself, Lucifer sowed the seeds of doubt in the minds of many of the angels.—*Educational Messenger*, Sept. 11, 1908.

His [Lucifer's] work of deception was done in so great secrecy that the angels in less exalted positions supposed that he was the Ruler of heaven.—TDG 256.

Angels that were loyal and true sought to reconcile this mighty, rebellious angel to the will of his Creator. They justified the act of God in conferring honor upon Jesus Christ, and with forcible reasoning sought to convince Satan that no less honor was his now than before the Father had proclaimed the honor which He had conferred upon His Son. They clearly set forth that Jesus was the Son of God, existing with Him before the angels were created; and that He had ever stood at the right hand of God, and His mild, loving authority had not heretofore been questioned; and that He had given no commands but what it was joy for the heavenly host to execute. They urged that Christ's receiving special honor from the Father, in the presence of the angels, did not detract from the honor that he [Satan] had heretofore received.—1SP 19.

He [Lucifer] gained the sympathy of some of his associates by suggesting thoughts of criticism regarding the government of God. This evil seed was scattered in a most seducing manner; and after it had sprung up and taken root in the minds of many, he gathered the ideas that he himself had first implanted in the minds of others, and brought them before the highest order of angels as the thoughts of other minds against the government of God.—4BC 1143.

Lucifer . . . at first so conducted his temptations that he himself stood uncommitted. The angels whom he could not bring fully to his side, he accused of indifference to the interests of heavenly beings. The very work which he himself was doing, he charged upon the loyal angels. It was his policy to perplex with subtle arguments concerning the purposes of God. Everything that was simple he shrouded in mystery, and by artful perversion cast doubt upon the plainest statements of Jehovah. And his high position, so closely connected with the divine government, gave greater force to his representations.—PP 41.

The very first effort of Satan to overthrow God's law—undertaken among the sinless inhabitants of heaven—seemed for a time to be crowned with success. A vast number of the angels were seduced. —PP 331.

God's government included not only the inhabitants of heaven but of all the created worlds; and Satan thought that if he could carry the intelligences of heaven with him in rebellion, he could also carry with him the other worlds.—RH March 9, 1886.

Here, for a time, Satan had the advantage; and he exulted in his arrogated superiority, in this one respect, to the angels of heaven, and even to God himself. . . . [Lucifer] had disguised himself in a cloak of falsehood, and for a time it was impossible to tear off the covering, so that the hideous deformity of his character could be seen. He must be left to reveal himself in his cruel, artful, wicked works.—4SP 319.

Lucifer Is Given Time to Develop His Principles

God in His wisdom did not immediately thrust Satan out of heaven. This act would not have changed his principles, and would only have strengthened his rebellion, for it would have created sympathy for him as one unjustly dealt with; and he would have carried a much larger number with him. He must be displaced, and have time to more fully develop his principles. —RH March 9, 1886.

Satan complained of the supposed defects in the management of heavenly things, and sought to fill the minds of the angels with his disaffection. Because he was not supreme, he sowed seeds of doubt and unbelief. Because he was not as God, he strove to instill into the minds of the angels his own envy and dissatisfaction. Thus the seeds of alienation were planted, afterward to be drawn out and presented before the heavenly courts as originating, not with Satan, but with the angels. So the deceiver would show that the angels thought as he did. . . .

That which Satan had instilled into the minds of the angels—a word here and a word there—opened the way for a long list of suppositions. In his artful way he drew expressions of doubt from them. Then, when he was interviewed, he accused those whom he had educated. He laid all the disaffection on the ones he had led.—RH Sept. 7, 1897.

He [Lucifer] began to insinuate doubts concerning the laws that governed heavenly beings, intimating that though laws might be necessary for the inhabitants of the worlds, angels, being more exalted, needed no such restraint, for their own wisdom was sufficient guide. —PP 37.

Lucifer . . . sought to abolish the law of God. He claimed that the unfallen intelligences of holy heaven had no need of law, but were capable of governing themselves and of preserving unspotted integrity.—ST April 28, 1890.

Even the loyal angels did not fully discern his [Satan's] character. This was why God did not at once destroy Satan. Had He done so, the holy angels would not have perceived the justice and love of God. A doubt of God's goodness would have been as evil seed that would yield the bitter fruit of sin and woe. Therefore the author of evil was spared, fully to develop his character.—COL 72.

The Angels Debate the Issues

While some of the angels joined Satan in his rebellion, others reasoned with him to dissuade him from his purposes, contending for the honor and wisdom of God in giving authority to His Son. Satan urged, for what reason was Christ endowed with unlimited power and such high command above himself!—3SG 37.

Satan refused to listen. And then he turned from the loyal and true angels, denouncing them as slaves. These angels, true to God, stood in amazement as they saw that Satan was successful in his efforts to excite rebellion. He promised them a new and better government than they then had, in which all would be freedom. Great numbers signified their purpose to accept Satan as their leader and chief commander. As he saw his advances were met with success, he flattered himself that he should yet have all the angels on his side, and that he would be equal with God Himself, and his voice of authority would be heard in commanding the entire host of heaven.

Again the loyal angels warned Satan and assured him what must be the consequence if he persisted; that He who could create the angels, could by His power overturn all their authority and terrible rebellion. To think that an angel should resist the law of God which was as sacred as Himself! They warned the rebellious to close their ears to Satan's deceptive reasonings, and advised Satan, and all who had been affected by him, to go to God and confess their wrong for even admitting a thought of questioning His authority.—1SP 20.

Satan was artful in presenting his side of the question. As soon as he found that one position was seen in its true character, he changed it for another. Not so with God. He could work with only one class of weapons—truth and righteousness. Satan could use what God could not—crookedness and deceit.—RH March 9, 1886.

The underworking [of Satan] was so subtle that it could not be made to appear before the heavenly host as the thing that it really was . . . . This condition of things had existed a long period of time before Satan was unmasked.—4BC 1143.

God in His great mercy bore long with Lucifer. He was not immediately degraded from his exalted station when he first indulged the spirit of discontent, not even when he began to present his false claims before the loyal angels. Long was he retained in heaven. Again and again he was offered pardon on condition of repentance and submission.—GC 495, 496.

The spirit of discontent and disaffection had never before been known in heaven. It was a new element, strange, mysterious, unaccountable. Lucifer himself had not at first been acquainted with the real nature of his feelings; for a time he had feared to express the workings and imaginings of his mind; yet he did not dismiss them. He did not see whither he was drifting. But such efforts as infinite love and wisdom only could devise, were made to convince him of his error. His disaffection was proved to be without cause, and he was made to see what would be the result of persisting in revolt. Lucifer was convinced that he was in the wrong. He saw that the divine statutes are just, and that he ought to acknowledge them as such before all heaven.

Had he done this, he might have saved himself and many angels. He had not at that time fully cast off his allegiance to God. Though he had left his position as covering cherub, yet if he had been willing to return to God, acknowledging the Creator's wisdom, and satisfied to fill the place appointed him in God's great plan, he would have been reinstated in his office. The time had come for a final decision; he must fully yield to the divine sovereignty or place himself in open rebellion. He nearly reached the decision to return, but pride forbade him.—PP 39.

God Meets Satan's Challenge

In the councils of heaven it was decided that principles must be acted upon that would not at once destroy Satan's power; for it was God's purpose to place things upon an eternal basis of security. Time must be given for Satan to develop the principles which were the foundation of his government. The heavenly universe must see worked out the principles which Satan declared to be superior to God's principles. God's order must be contrasted with Satan's order. The corrupting principles of Satan's rule must be revealed. The principles of righteousness expressed in God's law must be demonstrated as unchangeable, perfect, eternal.—RH Sept. 7, 1897.

The loyal angels hasten speedily to the Son of God and acquaint Him with what is taking place among the angels. They find the Father in conference with His beloved Son, to determine the means by which, for the best good of the loyal angels, the assumed authority of Satan could be forever put down. The great God could at once have hurled this arch deceiver from heaven;

but this was not His purpose. He would give the rebellious an equal chance to measure strength and might with His own Son and His loyal angels. In this battle every angel would choose his own side, and be manifested to all.—1SP 21.

Lucifer Becomes Satan

Satan . . . determined to make himself a center of influence. If he could not be the highest authority in heaven, he would be the highest authority in rebellion against the government of heaven. Head he would be, to control, not to be controlled.—RH April 16, 1901.

Many of Satan's sympathizers were inclined to heed the counsel of the loyal angels, and repent of their dissatisfaction, and be again received to the confidence of the Father and His dear Son. The mighty revolter then declared that he was acquainted with God's law, and if he should submit to servile obedience, his honor would be taken from him. No more would he be intrusted with his exalted mission. He told them that himself and they also had now gone too far to go back, and he would brave the consequences; for to bow in servile worship to the Son of God he never would; that God would not forgive, and now they must assert their liberty and gain by force the position and authority which was not willingly accorded them.—1SP 20, 21.

So far as Satan himself was concerned, it was true that he had now gone too far to return. But not so with those who had been blinded by his deceptions. To them the counsel and entreaties of the loyal angels opened a door of hope; and had they heeded the warning, they might have broken away from the snare of Satan. But pride, love for their leader, and the desire for unrestricted freedom were permitted to bear sway, and the pleadings of divine love and mercy were finally rejected.—PP 41.

The Angels Appear Before the Father

All the heavenly host were summoned to appear before the Father, to have each case determined. Satan unblushingly made known his dissatisfaction that Christ should be preferred before him. He stood up proudly and urged that he should be equal with God, and should be taken into conference with the Father and understand His purposes. God informed Satan that to His Son alone He would reveal His secret purposes, and He required all the family in heaven, even Satan, to yield Him implicit, unquestioned obedience; but that he had proved himself unworthy a place in heaven. Then Satan exultingly pointed to his sympathizers, comprising nearly one half of all the angels, and exclaimed, These are with me! Will you expel these also, and make such a void in heaven? He then declared that he was prepared to resist the authority of Christ, and to defend his place in heaven by force and might, strength against strength.—1SP 22.

To the very close of the controversy in heaven, the great usurper continued to justify himself. When it was announced that with all his sympathizers he must be expelled from the abodes of bliss, then the rebel leader boldly avowed his contempt for the Creator's law. He reiterated his claim that angels needed no control, but should be left to follow their own will, which would ever guide them right. He denounced the divine statutes as a restriction of their liberty, and declared that it was his purpose to secure the abolition of law; that, freed from this restraint, the hosts of heaven might enter upon a more exalted, more glorious state of existence.

With one accord, Satan and his host threw the blame of their rebellion wholly upon Christ, declaring that if they had not been reproved, they would never have rebelled.—GC 499, 500.

The knowledge which Satan, as well as the angels who fell with him, had of the character of God, of His goodness, His mercy, wisdom, and excellent glory, made their guilt unpardonable.—RH Feb. 24, 1874.

5.

The Rebellious Angels Are Cast Out, and Adam and Eve Fall

War in Heaven

Christ had worked in the heavenly courts to convince Satan of his terrible error, till at last the evil one and his sympathizers were found in open rebellion against God Himself.—TDG 256.

Christ, as Commander of heaven, was appointed to put down the rebellion.—RH May 30, 1899.

Then there was war in heaven. The Son of God, the Prince of Heaven, and His loyal angels, engaged in conflict with the arch rebel and those who united with him. The Son of God and true, loyal angels prevailed; and Satan and his sympathizers were expelled from heaven.—1SP 23.

Angels were engaged in the battle; Satan wished to conquer the Son of God and those who were submissive to His will. But the good and true angels prevailed, and Satan, with his followers, was driven from heaven.—EW 146.

The Effects of Rebellion

Satan stood in amazement at his new condition. His happiness was gone. He looked upon the angels who, with him, were once so happy, but who had been expelled from heaven. . . . Now all seemed changed. Countenances which had reflected the image of their Maker were gloomy and despairing. Strife, discord, and bitter recrimination, were among them. . . . Satan now beholds the terrible results of his rebellion. He shuddered, and feared to face the future, and to contemplate the end of these things.

The hour for joyful, happy songs of praise to God and His dear Son had come. Satan had led the heavenly choir. He had raised the first note, then all the angelic host united with him, and glorious strains of music had resounded through heaven in honor of God and His dear Son. But now, instead of strains of sweetest music, discord and angry words fall upon the ear of the great rebel leader. . . . The hour of worship draws nigh, when bright and holy angels bow before the Father. No more will he unite in heavenly song. No more will he bow in reverence and holy awe before the presence of the eternal God. . . .

Satan trembled as he viewed his work. He was alone in meditation upon the past, the present, and his future plans. His mighty frame shook as with a tempest. An angel from heaven was passing. He called him, and entreated an interview with Christ. This was granted him. He then related to the Son of God that he repented of his rebellion, and wished again the favor of God. He was willing to take the place God had previously assigned him, and be under his wise command. Christ wept at Satan's woe, but told him, as the mind of God, that he could never be received into heaven. . . . The seeds of rebellion were still within him. . . .

When Satan became fully convinced that there was no possibility of his being reinstated in the favor of God, he manifested his malice with increased hatred and fiery vehemence. . . .

As he could not gain admission within the gates of heaven, he would wait just at the entrance, to taunt the angels and seek contention with them as they went in and out.—1SP 28-30.

The Creation of Earth and Humankind

The loyal angels mourned the fate of those who had been their companions in happiness and bliss. Their loss was felt in heaven. The Father consulted Jesus in regard to at once carrying out their purpose to make man to inhabit the earth.—ST Jan. 9, 1879.

The brightest and most exalted of the sons of the morning heralded . . . [Christ's] glory at creation, and announced His birth with songs of gladness.—ST Jan. 4, 1883.

When God formed the earth, there were mountains, hills, and plains, and interspersed among them were rivers and bodies of water. The earth was not one extensive plain, but the monotony of the scenery was broken by hills and mountains, not high and ragged as they are now, but regular and beautiful in shape. . . .

Angels beheld and rejoiced at the wonderful and beautiful works of God.—3SG 33.

All heaven took a deep and joyful interest in the creation of the world and of man. Human beings were a new and distinct order.—RH Feb. 11, 1902.

Next to the angelic beings, the human family, formed in the image of God, are the noblest of His created works.—RH Dec. 3, 1908.

The Lord . . . had endowed Adam with powers of mind superior to any living creature that He had made. His mental powers were but little lower than those of the angels.—RH Feb. 24, 1874.

As soon as the Lord through Jesus Christ created our world, and placed Adam and Eve in the garden of Eden, Satan announced his purpose to conform to his own nature the father and mother of all humanity. —RH April 14, 1896.

When the Lord presented Eve to Adam, angels of God were witnesses to the ceremony.—HP 203.

This sinless pair wore no artificial garments. They were clothed with a covering of light and glory, such as the angels wear.—ST Jan. 9, 1879.

God created man for His own glory, that after test and trial the human family might become one with the heavenly family. It was God's purpose to repopulate heaven with the human family.—1BC 1082.

The vacancies made in heaven by the fall of Satan and his angels will be filled by the redeemed of the Lord.—RH May 29, 1900.

Adam and Eve in Eden

Although everything God had made was in the perfection of beauty, and there seemed nothing wanting upon the earth which God had created to make Adam and Eve happy, yet He manifested His great love to them by planting a garden especially for them. A portion of their time was to be occupied in the happy employment of dressing the garden, and a portion in receiving the visits of angels, listening to their instruction, and in happy meditation. Their labor was not wearisome, but pleasant and invigorating.—ST Jan. 9, 1879.

Holy angels . . . gave instruction to Adam and Eve concerning their employment, and also taught them concerning the rebellion of Satan and his fall.—1SG 20.

He [Adam] stood before God in the strength of perfect manhood, all the organs and faculties of his being fully developed and harmoniously balanced; and he was surrounded with things of beauty, and conversed daily with the holy angels.—2SP 88.

The law of God existed before man was created. It was adapted to the condition of holy beings; even angels were governed by it.—ST April 15, 1886.

Man was to be tested and proved, and if he should bear the test of God, and remain loyal and true after the first trial, he was not to be beset with continual temptations; but was to be exalted equal with the angels, and henceforth immortal.—RH Feb. 24, 1874.

Satan Plans to Cause Man's Fall

He [Satan] . . . informed them [his angel followers] of his plans to wrest from God the noble Adam and his companion Eve. If he could, in any way, beguile them to disobedience, God would make some provision whereby they might be pardoned, and then himself and all the fallen angels would be in a fair way to share with them of God's mercy. If this should fail, they could unite with Adam and Eve; for when once they should transgress the law of God, they would be subjects of God's wrath, like themselves. Their transgression would place them also in a state of rebellion; and they could unite with Adam and Eve, take possession of Eden, and hold it as their home. And if they could gain access to the tree of life in the midst of the garden, their strength would, they thought, be equal to that of the holy angels, and even God Himself could not expel them.

Satan held a consultation with his evil angels. They did not all readily unite to engage in this hazardous and terrible work. He told them that he would not intrust any one of them to accomplish this work; for he thought that he alone had wisdom sufficient to carry forward so important an enterprise. He wished them to consider the matter while he should leave them and seek retirement, to mature his plans. . . .

Satan went alone to mature plans that would most surely secure the fall of Adam and Eve. He shuddered at the thought of plunging the holy, happy pair into the misery and remorse he was himself enduring. He seemed in a state of indecision; at one time firm and determined, then hesitating and wavering. His angels were seeking him, their leader, to acquaint him with their decision. They will unite with Satan in his plans, and with him bear the responsibility, and share the consequences.

Satan cast off his feelings of despair and weakness, and, as their leader, fortified himself to brave out the matter, and do all in his power to defy the authority of God and His Son.—1SP 31-33.

Satan declared that he would prove to the worlds which God has created, and to the heavenly intelligences, that it was an impossibility to keep the law of God.—RH Sept. 3, 1901.

God assembled the angelic host to take measures to avert the threatened evil. It was decided in Heaven's council for angels to visit Eden and warn Adam that he was in danger from the foe. Accordingly, two angels sped on their way to visit our first parents.—ST Jan. 16, 1879.

Heavenly messengers opened to them [Adam and Eve] the history of Satan's fall, and his plots for their destruction, unfolding more fully the nature of the divine government, which the prince of evil was trying to overthrow. . . .

The angels warned them to be on their guard against the devices of Satan; for his efforts to ensnare them would be unwearied. While they were obedient to God, the evil one could not harm them; for, if need be, every angel in heaven would be sent to their help. If they steadfastly repelled his first insinuations, they would be as secure as the heavenly messengers. But should they once yield to temptation, their nature would become so depraved that in themselves they would have no power, and no disposition, to resist Satan.—PP 52, 53.

The angels cautioned Eve not to separate from her husband in her employment; for she might be brought in contact with this fallen foe. If separated from each other, they would be in greater danger than if both were together. The angels charged them to closely follow the instructions God had given them in reference to the tree of knowledge; for in perfect obedience they were safe, and this fallen foe could have access to them only at the tree of knowledge of good and evil.

Adam and Eve assured the angels that they should never transgress the express command of God; for it was their highest pleasure to do His will. The angels united with Adam and Eve in holy strains of harmonious music; and as their songs pealed forth from blissful Eden, Satan heard the sound of their strains of joyful adoration to the Father and Son. And as Satan heard it, his envy, hatred, and malignity increased, and he expressed his anxiety to his followers to incite them (Adam and Eve) to disobedience.—1SP 34, 35.

Satan Speaks to Eve Through a Serpent

In order to accomplish his work unperceived, Satan

chose to employ as his medium the serpent—a disguise well adapted for his purpose of deception. The serpent was then one of the wisest and most beautiful creatures on the earth. It had wings, and while flying through the air presented an appearance of dazzling brightness, having the color and brilliancy of burnished gold.—PP 53.

Eve went from the side of her husband, viewing the beautiful things of nature in God's creation, delighting her senses with the colors and fragrance of the flowers and the beauty of the trees and shrubs. She was thinking of the restriction God had laid upon them in regard to the tree of knowledge. She was pleased with the beauties and bounties which the Lord had furnished for the gratification of every want. All these, said she, God has given us to enjoy. They are all ours; for God has said, "Of every tree of the garden thou mayest freely eat; but of the tree of the knowledge of good and evil, thou shalt not eat of it."

Eve had wandered near the forbidden tree, and her curiosity was aroused to know how death could be concealed in the fruit of this fair tree. She was surprised to hear her queries taken up and repeated by a strange voice. "Yea, hath God said, Ye shall not eat of every tree of the garden?" Eve was not aware that she had revealed her thoughts by conversing to herself aloud, therefore she was greatly astonished to hear her queries repeated by a serpent.—RH Feb. 24, 1874.

With soft and pleasant words, and with musical voice, he [Satan] addressed the wondering Eve. She was startled to hear a serpent speak. He extolled her beauty and exceeding loveliness, which was not displeasing to Eve.

Eve was beguiled, flattered, infatuated.—1SP 35, 36.

She [Eve] really thought the serpent had a knowledge of her thoughts, and that he must be very wise. She answered him, "We may eat of the fruit of the trees of the garden; but of the fruit of the tree which is in the midst of the garden, God hath said, Ye shall not eat of it, neither shall ye touch it, lest ye die. And the serpent said unto the woman, Ye shall not surely die; for God doth know that in the day ye eat thereof, then your eyes shall be opened, and ye shall be as gods, knowing good and evil." [Gen. 3:2-5.]

Here the father of lies made his assertion in direct contradiction to the expressed word of God. Satan assured Eve that she was created immortal, and that there was no possibility of her dying. He told her that God knew that if they ate of the tree of knowledge their understanding would be enlightened, expanded, and ennobled, making them equal with Himself. . . . Eve thought the discourse of the serpent very wise. . . . She looked with longing desire upon the tree laden with fruit which appeared very delicious. The serpent was eating it with apparent delight.

Eve had overstated the words of God's command. He had said to Adam and Eve, "But of the tree of the knowledge of good and evil thou shalt not eat of it, for in the day thou eatest thereof thou shalt surely die." In Eve's controversy with the serpent, she added the clause, *"Neither shall ye touch it, lest ye die."* Here the subtlety of the serpent was seen. This statement of Eve gave him advantage.—RH Feb. 24, 1874.

By partaking of this tree, he [Satan] declared they would attain to a more exalted sphere of existence, and enter a broader field of knowledge. He himself had eaten of the forbidden fruit, and as a result had acquired the power of speech. And he insinuated that the Lord jealously desired to withhold it from them, lest they should be exalted to equality with Himself.—PP 54.

Eve's curiosity was aroused. Instead of fleeing from the spot, she listened to hear a serpent talk. It did not occur to her mind that it might be that fallen foe, using the serpent as a medium.—1SP 36.

With what intense interest the whole universe watched the conflict that was to decide the position of Adam and Eve. How attentively the angels listened to the words of Satan, the originator of sin, as he placed his own ideas above the commands of God, and sought to make of none effect the law of God through his deceptive reasoning! How anxiously they waited to see if the holy pair would be deluded by the tempter, and yield to his arts. . . .

Satan represented God as a deceiver, as one who would debar His creatures from the benefit of His highest gift. The angels heard with sorrow and amazement this statement in regard to the character of God, as Satan represented Him as possessing his own miserable attributes; but Eve was not horror-stricken to hear the holy and supreme God thus falsely accused. If she had . . .

remembered all the tokens of His love, if she had fled to her husband, she might have been saved from the subtle temptation of the evil one.—ST May 12, 1890.

The tempter plucked the fruit and passed it to Eve. She took it in her hand. Now, said the tempter, you were prohibited from even touching it lest you die. He told her that she would realize no more sense of evil and death in eating than in touching or handling the fruit. Eve was emboldened because she felt not the immediate signs of God's displeasure. She thought the words of the tempter all wise and correct. She ate, and was delighted with the fruit. It seemed delicious to her taste, and she imagined that she realized in herself the wonderful effects of the fruit.—1SP 38.

There was nothing poisonous in the fruit of the tree of knowledge itself, nothing that would cause death in partaking of it. The tree had been placed in the garden to test their loyalty to God.—ST Feb. 13, 1896.

Eve Eats the Fruit and Tempts Adam

Eve ate and imagined that she felt the sensations of a new and more exalted life. . . . She felt no ill effects from the fruit, nothing which could be interpreted to mean death, but, just as the serpent had said, a pleasurable sensation which she imagined was as the angels felt.—3T 72.

She then plucked for herself of the fruit and ate, and imagined she felt the quickening power of a new and elevated existence as the result of the exhilarating influence of the forbidden fruit. She was in a strange and unnatural excitement as she sought her husband, with her hands filled with the forbidden fruit. She related to him the wise discourse of the serpent, and wished to conduct him at once to the tree of knowledge. She told him she had eaten of the fruit, and instead of her feeling any sense of death, she realized a pleasing, exhilarating influence. As soon as Eve had disobeyed, she became a powerful medium through which to occasion the fall of her husband.—1SP 38, 39.

An expression of sadness came over the face of Adam. He appeared astonished and alarmed. To the words of Eve he replied that this must be the foe against whom they had been warned; and by the divine sentence she must die. In answer she urged him to eat, repeating the words of the serpent, that they should not surely die. She reasoned that this must be true, for she felt no evidence of God's displeasure. . . .

Adam understood that his companion had transgressed the command of God, disregarded the only prohibition laid upon them as a test of their fidelity and love. There was a terrible struggle in his mind. He mourned that he had permitted Eve to wander from his side. But now the deed was done; he must be separated from her whose society had been his joy. How could he have it thus? He resolved to share her fate; if she must die, he would die with her. After all, he reasoned, might not the words of the wise serpent be true? Eve was before him, as beautiful, and apparently as innocent, as before this act of disobedience. She expressed greater love for him than before. No sign of death appeared in her, and he decided to brave the consequences. He seized the fruit, and quickly ate.

After his transgression, Adam at first imagined himself entering upon a higher state of existence. But soon the thought of his sin filled him with terror. The air, which had hitherto been of a mild and uniform temperature, seemed to chill the guilty pair. The love and peace which had been theirs was gone, and in its place they felt a sense of sin, a dread of the future, a nakedness of soul.—PP 56, 57.

Satan exulted in his success. He had now tempted the woman to distrust God, to question His wisdom, and to seek to penetrate His all-wise plans. And through her he had also caused the overthrow of Adam, who, in consequence of his love for Eve, disobeyed the command of God, and fell with her.—1SP 42.

Satan, the fallen angel, had declared that no man could keep God's law, and he pointed to the disobedience of Adam as proving the declaration true.—ST April 10, 1893.

Satan . . . proudly boasted that the world which God had made was his dominion. Having conquered Adam, the monarch of the world, he had gained the race as his subjects, and he should now possess Eden, and make that his headquarters. And he would there establish his throne, and be monarch of the world.—RH Feb. 24, 1874.

The Council of Peace

The news of man's fall spread through heaven—every harp was hushed. The angels cast their crowns from their heads in sorrow. All heaven was in agitation. —1SP 42.

A council was held to decide what must be done with the guilty pair.—3SG 44.

The anxiety of the angels seemed to be intense while Jesus was communing with His Father. Three times He was shut in by the glorious light about the Father, and the third time He came from the Father, His person could be seen. . . . He then made known to the angelic host that a way of escape had been made for lost man. He told them that He had been pleading with His Father, and had offered to give His life a ransom, to take the sentence of death upon Himself, that through Him man might find pardon. . . .

At first the angels could not rejoice; for their Commander concealed nothing from them, but opened before them the plan of salvation. Jesus told them that He would . . . leave all His glory in heaven, appear upon earth as a man, humble Himself as a man, . . . and that finally, after His mission as a teacher would be accomplished, He would be delivered into the hands of men, and endure almost every cruelty and suffering that Satan and his angels could inspire men to inflict; that He would die the cruelest of deaths, hung up between the heavens and the earth as a guilty sinner; that He should suffer dreadful hours of agony, which even angels could not look upon, but would veil their faces from the sight. . . .

The angels prostrated themselves before Him. They offered their lives. Jesus said to them that He would by His death save many; that the life of an angel could not pay the debt. His life alone could be accepted of the Father as a ransom for man.—EW 149, 150.

The angels feared that they [Adam and Eve] would put forth the hand, and eat of the tree of life, and be immortal sinners. But God said that He would drive the transgressors from the garden. Angels were commissioned immediately to guard the way of the tree of life.—1SG 22.

The angels who had been appointed to guard Adam in his Eden home before his transgression and expulsion from paradise were now appointed to guard the gates of paradise and the way of the tree of life.—RH Feb. 24, 1874.

When Adam and Eve realized how exalted and sacred was the law of God, the transgression of which made so costly a sacrifice necessary to save them and their posterity from utter ruin, they pled to die themselves, or to let them and their posterity endure the penalty of their transgression, rather than that the beloved Son of God should make this great sacrifice. . . .

Adam was informed that an angel's life could not pay the debt. The law of Jehovah, the foundation of His government in heaven and upon earth, was as sacred as God Himself; and for this reason the life of an angel could not be accepted of God as a sacrifice for its transgression. . . . The Father could not abolish nor change one precept of His law to meet man in his fallen condition. But the Son of God, who had in unison with the Father created man, could make an atonement for man acceptable to God. . . .

When Adam, according to God's special directions, made an offering for sin, it was to him a most painful ceremony. His hand must be raised to take life, which God alone could give, and make an offering for sin. It was the first time he had witnessed death. As he looked upon the bleeding victim, writhing in the agonies of death, he was to look forward by faith to the Son of God, whom the victim prefigured.—1SP 50-53.

Adam and Eve Expelled From Eden

They [Adam and Eve] were informed that they would have to lose their Eden home. . . . It was not safe for them to remain in the garden of Eden, lest in their state of sin, they gain access to the tree of life.—1SP 44.

They [Adam and Eve] earnestly entreated that they might remain in the home of their innocence and joy. They confessed that they had forfeited all right to that happy abode, but pledged themselves for the future to yield strict obedience to God. But they were told that their nature had become depraved by sin; they had lessened their strength to resist evil, and had opened the way for Satan to gain more ready access to them. In their innocence they had yielded to temptation; and now, in a state of conscious guilt, they would have less power to maintain their integrity.

In humility and unutterable sadness they bade farewell to their beautiful home, and went forth to dwell upon the earth, where rested the curse of sin.—PP 61.

Holy angels were sent to drive out the disobedient pair from the garden, while other angels guarded the way to the tree of life. Each one of these mighty angels had in his right hand a glittering sword.—3SG 45.

Strong angels, with beams of light representing flaming swords turning in every direction, were placed as sentinels to guard the way of the tree of life from the approach of Satan and the guilty pair.—RH Feb. 24, 1874.

It was Satan's studied plan that Adam and Eve should disobey God, receive His frown, and then partake of the tree of life, that they might perpetuate a life of sin. But holy angels were sent to debar their way to the tree of life. Around these angels flashed beams of light on every side, which had the appearance of glittering swords.—1SP 44.

After the fall, Satan bade his angels make special effort to foster the belief in man's natural immortality; and when they had induced the people to receive this error, they led them to conclude that the sinner would live in eternal misery.—4SP 354.

6.

Angels Before and After Noah's Flood

The Plan of Salvation Explained Further

Angels held communication with Adam after his fall, and informed him of the plan of salvation, and that the human race was not beyond redemption.—3SG 52.

Angels informed Adam that, as his transgression had brought death and wretchedness, life and immortality would be brought to light through the sacrifice of Jesus Christ.—1SP 51.

The garden of Eden remained upon the earth long after man had become an outcast from its pleasant paths. The fallen race were long permitted to gaze upon the home of innocence, their entrance barred only by the watching angels.—PP 62.

Worship at the Cherubim-guarded Gate

At the cherubim-guarded gate of Paradise the glory of the Lord was revealed, and hither came the first worshipers. . . . It was here that Cain and Abel had brought their sacrifices, and God had condescended to communicate with them.

Skepticism could not deny the existence of Eden while it stood just in sight, its entrance barred by watching angels. The order of creation, the object of the garden, the history of its two trees so closely connected with man's destiny, were undisputed facts. And the existence and supreme authority of God, the obligation to His law, were truths which men were slow to question while Adam was among them.—PP 83, 84.

[Cain and Abel] had been instructed in regard to the provision made for the salvation of the human race. They were required to carry out a system of humble obedience, showing their reverence for God, and their faith and dependence upon the promised Redeemer, by slaying the firstlings of the flock, and solemnly presenting it with the blood, as a burnt offering to God. . . .

He [Cain] was unwilling to strictly follow the plan of obedience, and procure a lamb and offer it with the fruit of the ground. He merely took of the fruit of the ground and disregarded the requirement of God. . . . Abel advised his brother not to come before the Lord without the blood of a sacrifice. Cain being the eldest, would not listen to his brother. . . .

Abel brought of the firstlings of his flock, and of the fat as God had commanded; and in full faith of the Messiah to come, and with humble reverence, he presented the offering. God had respect unto his offering. A light flashes from heaven and consumes the offering of Abel. Cain sees no manifestation that his is accepted. He is angry with the Lord, and with his brother. God condescends to send an angel to Cain to converse with him.

The angel inquires of him the reason of his anger, and informs him that if he does well, and follows the directions God has given, He will accept him, and respect his offering. But if he will not humbly submit to God's arrangements, and believe and obey Him, He cannot accept his offering. The angel tells Cain that it was no injustice on the part of God, or partiality shown to Abel; but that it was on account of his own sin, and disobedience of God's express command, why He could not respect his offering—and if he would do well he would be accepted of God. . . . But even after being thus faithfully instructed, Cain did not repent. . . . In his jealousy and hatred he contends with Abel, and reproaches him. . . . While Abel justifies the plan of God, Cain becomes enraged, and his anger increases and burns against Abel, until in his rage he slays him. —3SG 47-49.

Adam and Angels Instructed Antediluvians

The advantages enjoyed by men of that age [pre-Flood] to gain a knowledge of God through His works have never been equaled since. And so far from being an era of religious darkness, that was an age of great light. All the world had opportunity to receive instruction from Adam, and those who feared the Lord had also Christ and angels for their teachers.—PP 83.

Men lived nearly a thousand years in those days [before the Flood], and angels visited them with instruction directly from Christ.—1SM 230.

Enoch

Enoch learned from the lips of Adam the painful story of the fall, and the precious story of God's condescending grace in the gift of His Son as the world's Redeemer. He believed and relied upon the promise given. Enoch was a holy man. He served God with singleness of heart. He realized the corruptions of the human family, and separated himself from the descendants of Cain, and reproved them for their great wickedness. . . . His soul was vexed as he daily beheld them trampling upon the authority of God. . . . He chose to be separate from them and spent much of his time in solitude, giving himself to reflection and prayer. He waited before God, and prayed to know His will more perfectly, that he might perform it. God communed with Enoch through His angels, and gave him divine instruction. He made known to him that He would not always bear with man in his rebellion—that it was His purpose to destroy the sinful race by bringing a flood of waters upon the earth.

The Lord opened more fully to Enoch the plan of salvation, and by the Spirit of prophecy carried him down through the generations which should live after the flood, and showed him the great events connected with the second coming of Christ and the end of the world.

Enoch was troubled in regard to the dead. It seemed to him that the righteous and the wicked would go to the dust together, and that would be their end. He could not see the life of the just beyond the grave. In prophetic vision he was instructed in regard to the Son of God, who was to die man's sacrifice, and was shown the coming of Christ in the clouds of heaven, attended by the angelic host, to give life to the righteous dead, and ransom them from their graves. . . .

Enoch faithfully rehearsed to the people all that had been revealed to him by the Spirit of prophecy. Some believed his words, and turned from their wickedness to fear and worship God.—ST Feb. 20, 1879.

He [Enoch] chose certain periods for retirement, and would not suffer the people to find him, for they interrupted his holy meditation and communion with God. He did not exclude himself at all times from the society of those who loved him and listened to his words of wisdom; neither did he separate himself wholly from the corrupt. He met with the good and bad at stated times, and labored to turn the ungodly from their evil course.—3SG 56.

Enoch continued to grow more heavenly while communing with God. . . . The Lord loved Enoch, because he steadfastly followed Him, and abhorred iniquity, and earnestly sought a more perfect knowledge of His will that he might perform it. He yearned to unite himself still more closely to God, whom he feared, reverenced, and adored. The Lord would not permit Enoch to die like other men, but sent His angels to take him to heaven without seeing death. In the presence of the righteous and the wicked, Enoch was removed from them. Those who loved him thought that God might have left him in some of his places of retirement; but after seeking diligently, and being unable to find him, they reported that he was not, for God took him.—ST Feb. 20, 1879.

The flaming chariots of God were sent for this holy man, and he was borne to heaven.—RH April 19, 1870.

The Lord has given me a view of other worlds. Wings were given me, and an angel attended me from the city to a place that was bright and glorious. . . . Then I was taken to a world which had seven moons. There I saw good old Enoch, who had been translated. On his right arm he bore a glorious palm, and on each leaf was written "Victory." Around his head was a dazzling white wreath, and leaves on the wreath, and in the middle of each leaf was written "Purity," and around the wreath were stones of various colors, that shone brighter than the stars, and cast a reflection upon the letters and magnified them. On the back part of his head was a bow that confined the wreath, and upon the bow was written "Holiness." Above the wreath was a lovely crown that shone brighter than the sun. I asked him if this was the place he was taken to from the earth. He said, "It is not; the city is my home, and I have come to visit this place."—EW 39, 40.

Enoch represents those who shall remain upon the earth and be translated to heaven without seeing death. He represents that company that are to live amid the perils of the last days, and withstand all the corruption, vileness, sin, and iniquity, and yet be unsullied by it all. We can stand as did Enoch. There has been provision made for us. . . . Angels of God that excel in strength, are sent to minister to those who shall be heirs of salvation. These angels, when they see that we are doing the very utmost on our part to be overcomers, will do their part, and their light will shine around about us, and sway back the influence of the evil angels that are around us, and will make a fortification around us as a wall of fire.—RH April 19, 1870.

Noah

Those who lived in the days of Noah and Abraham were more like the angels in form, in comeliness and strength. But every generation has been growing weaker.—1SG 69.

More than one hundred years before the flood the Lord sent an angel to faithful Noah to make known to him that He would no longer have mercy upon the corrupt race. But He would not have them ignorant of His design. He would instruct Noah, and make him a faithful preacher to warn the world of its coming destruction, that the inhabitants of the earth might be left without excuse. . . .

Angels were sent to collect from the forest and field the beasts which God had created.—1SP 69, 72.

Angels went before these animals and they followed two and two, male and female, and clean beasts by sevens.—3SG 67.

Everything was now ready for the closing of the ark, which could not have been done by Noah from within. An angel is seen by the scoffing multitude descending from heaven, clothed with brightness like the lightning. He closes that massive outer door, and then takes his course upward to heaven again.—1SP 72.

The Flood Comes

Notwithstanding the solemn exhibition they [the antediluvians] had witnessed of God's power—of the unnatural occurrence of the beasts' leaving the forests and fields, and going into the ark, and the angel of God clothed with brightness, and terrible in majesty, descending from heaven and closing the door; yet they hardened their hearts, and continued to revel and sport over the signal manifestations of divine power. But upon the eighth day the heavens gathered blackness. . . . The rain descended from the clouds above them. This was something they had never witnessed. . . . The storm increased in violence until water seemed to come from heaven like mighty cataracts. . . . Jets of water would burst up from the earth with indescribable force, throwing massive rocks hundreds of feet into the air, and then they would bury themselves deep in the earth. . . .

The violence of the storm increased, and there were mingled with the warring of the elements the wailings of the people who had despised the authority of God. Trees, buildings, rocks, and earth were hurled in every direction. The terror of man and beast was beyond description. And even Satan himself, who was compelled to be amid the warring elements, feared for his own existence. . . .

Angels that excel in strength guided the ark and preserved it from harm. Every moment during that frightful storm of forty days and forty nights the preservation of the ark was a miracle of almighty power. —1SP 73, 75.

After the Flood

Anxiously did Noah and his family watch the decrease of the waters. He desired to go forth upon the earth again. He sent out a raven which flew back and forth to and from the ark. He did not receive the information he desired, and he sent forth a dove which, finding no rest, returned to the ark again. After seven days the dove was sent forth again, and when the olive leaf was seen in its mouth, there was great rejoicing by this family of eight, which had so long been shut up in the ark. Again an angel descends and opens the door of the ark. Noah could remove the top, but he could not open the door which God had shut. God spoke to Noah through the angel who opened the door, and bade the family of Noah go forth out of the ark, and bring forth with them every living thing. . . .

After Noah had come forth from the ark, he looked around upon the powerful and ferocious beasts which he brought out of the ark, and then upon his family numbering eight, and was greatly afraid that they would be destroyed by the beasts. But the Lord sent His angel to say to Noah, "The fear of you, and the dread of you, shall be upon every beast of the earth, and upon every fowl of the air, upon all that moveth upon the earth, and upon all the fishes of the sea; into your hands are they delivered. Every moving thing that liveth shall be meat for you; even as the green herb have I given you all things."—1SP 76, 78, 79.

The Builders of Babel

Some of the descendants of Noah soon began to apostatize. . . . Some disbelieved in the existence of God. . . . Others believed that God existed. . . . Those who were enemies of God felt daily reproved by the righteous conversation and godly lives of those who loved, obeyed, and exalted God. The unbelieving consulted among themselves and agreed to separate from the faithful. . . . They journeyed a distance from them, and selected a large plain wherein to dwell. They built them a city, and then conceived the idea of building a large tower to reach unto the clouds, that they might . . . be no more scattered. . . . They would build their tower to a much greater height than the waters prevailed in the time of the Flood . . . and they would be as gods and rule over the people. . . .

They exalted themselves against God. But He would not permit them to complete their work. They had built their tower to a lofty height, when the Lord sent two angels to confound them in their work. . . . The angels confounded their language. . . . After this, there was no harmony in their work. Angry with one another and unable to account for the misunderstanding, and strange words among them, they left the work and separated from each other, and scattered abroad in the earth. Up to this time, men had spoken but one language. Lightning from heaven, as a token of God's wrath, broke off the top of their tower, casting it to the ground.—1SP 91-93.

7.

Angels in the Patriarchal Age

Abraham

God conferred great honor upon Abraham. Angels of heaven walked and talked with him as friend with friend.—PP 138.

The Lord communicated His will to Abraham through angels. Christ appeared to him, and gave him a distinct knowledge of the requirements of the moral law, and of the great salvation which would be accomplished through Himself.—RH April 29, 1875.

After the birth of Ishmael, the Lord manifested Himself again to Abraham, and said unto him, "I will establish my covenant between me and thee, and thy seed after thee, in their generations, for an everlasting covenant." Again the Lord repeated by His angel His promise to give Sarah a son, and that she should be a mother of many nations.—1SP 96.

When judgments were about to be visited upon Sodom, the fact was not hidden from him, and he became an intercessor with God for sinners. His interview with the angels presents also a beautiful example of hospitality.

In the hot summer noontide the patriarch was sitting in his tent door, looking out over the quiet landscape, when he saw in the distance three travelers approaching. Before reaching his tent, the strangers halted, as if consulting as to their course. Without waiting for them to solicit favors, Abraham rose quickly, and as they were apparently turning in another direction, he hastened after them, and with the utmost courtesy urged them to honor him by tarrying for refreshment. With his own hands he brought water that they might wash the dust of travel from their feet. He himself selected their food, and while they were at rest under the cooling shade, an entertainment was made ready, and he stood respectfully beside them while they partook of his hospitality. . . .

Abraham had seen in his guests only three tired wayfarers, little thinking that among them was One whom he might worship without sin. But the true character of the heavenly messengers was now revealed. Though they were on their way as ministers of wrath, yet to Abraham, the man of faith, they spoke first of blessings. . . .

Abraham had honored God, and the Lord honored him, taking him into His counsels, and revealing to him His purposes. . . . God knew well the measure of Sodom's guilt; but He expressed Himself after the manner of men, that the justice of His dealings might be understood. Before bringing judgment upon the transgressors, He would go Himself to institute an examination of their course; if they had not passed the limits of divine mercy, He would still grant them space for repentance.—PP 138, 139.

The Destruction of Sodom and Gomorrah

Two of the heavenly messengers departed, leaving Abraham alone with Him whom he now knew to be the Son of God. . . . With deep reverence and humility he urged his plea: "I have taken upon me to speak unto the Lord, which am but dust and ashes." . . . He came close to the heavenly messenger, and fervently urged his petition. Though Lot had become a dweller in Sodom, he did not partake in the iniquity of its inhabitants. Abraham thought that in that populous city there must be other worshipers of the true God. And in view of this he pleaded, "That be far from thee, to do after this manner, to slay the righteous with the wicked; . . . that be far from thee. Shall not the Judge of all the earth do right?" Abraham asked not once merely, but many times. Waxing bolder as his requests were granted, he continued until he gained the assurance that if even ten righteous persons could be found in it, the city would be spared.—PP 139, 140.

Two Angels Visit Lot

In the twilight, two strangers drew near to the city gate. They were apparently travelers coming in to tarry for the night. None could discern in those humble wayfarers the mighty heralds of divine judgment, and little dreamed the pleasure-seeking, careless multitude that in their treatment of these heavenly messengers that very night they would reach the climax of the guilt which doomed their proud city. But there was one man who manifested kindly attention toward the strangers, and invited them to his home. Lot did not know their true character, but politeness and hospitality were habitual with him. —PP 158.

The angels revealed to Lot the object of their mission: "We will destroy this place, because the cry of them is waxen great before the face of the Lord; and the Lord hath sent us to destroy it." The strangers whom Lot had endeavored to protect, now promised to protect him, and to save also all the members of his family who would flee with him from the wicked city. . . . Lot went out to warn his children. He repeated the words of the angels, "Up, get you out of this place; for the Lord will destroy this city." But he seemed to them as one that mocked. . . .

Lot returned sorrowfully to his home, and told the story of his failure. Then the angels bade him arise, and take his wife and two daughters who were yet in his house, and leave the city. . . . Stupefied with sorrow, he lingered, loath to depart. But for the angels of God, they would all have perished in the ruin of Sodom. The heavenly messengers took him and his wife and daughters by the hand, and led them out of the city.

Here the angels left them, and turned back to Sodom to accomplish their work of destruction. Another— He with whom Abraham had pleaded—drew near to Lot. . . .

The Prince of heaven was by his side, yet he pleaded for his own life as though God, who had manifested such care and love for him, would not still preserve him. He should have trusted himself wholly to the divine Messenger, giving his will and his life into the Lord's hands without a doubt or a question. But like so many others, he endeavored to plan for himself. . . .

Again the solemn command was given to hasten, for the fiery storm would be delayed but little longer. But one of the fugitives [Lot's wife] ventured to cast a look backward to the doomed city, and she became a monument of God's judgment.—PP 158-161.

Abraham Tested

When Abraham was nearly one hundred years old, the promise of a son was repeated to him, with the assurance that the future heir should be the child of Sarah. . . . The birth of Isaac, bringing, after a life-long waiting, the fulfillment of their dearest hopes, filled the tents of Abraham and Sarah with gladness. . . .

Sarah saw in Ishmael's turbulent disposition a perpetual source of discord, and she appealed to Abraham, urging that Hagar and Ishmael be sent away from the encampment. The patriarch was thrown into great distress. How could he banish Ishmael his son, still dearly beloved? In his perplexity he pleaded for divine guidance. The Lord, through a holy angel, directed him to grant Sarah's desire. . . . And the angel gave him the consoling promise that though separated from his father's home, Ishmael should not be forsaken by God; his life should be preserved, and he should become the father of a great nation. Abraham obeyed the angel's

word, but it was not without keen suffering.
—PP 146, 147.

God had called Abraham to be the father of the faithful, and his life was to stand as an example of faith to succeeding generations. But his faith had not been perfect. . . . That he might reach the highest standard, God subjected him to another test, the closest which man was ever called to endure. In a vision of the night he was directed to repair to the land of Moriah, and there offer up his son as a burnt offering upon a mountain that should be shown him. . . .

The command was expressed in words that must have wrung with anguish that father's heart: "Take now thy son, thine only son Isaac, whom thou lovest, . . . and offer him for a burnt offering." Isaac was the light of his home, the solace of his old age, above all else the inheritor of the promised blessing. . . .

Satan was at hand to suggest that he must be deceived, for the divine law commands, "Thou shalt not kill," and God would not require what He had once forbidden. Going outside his tent, Abraham looked up to the calm brightness of the unclouded heavens, and recalled the promise made nearly fifty years before, that his seed should be innumerable as the stars. If this promise was to be fulfilled through Isaac, how could he be put to death? Abraham was tempted to believe that he might be under a delusion. . . . He remembered the angels sent to reveal to him God's purpose to destroy Sodom, and who bore to him the promise of this same son Isaac, and he went to the place where he had several times met the heavenly messengers, hoping to meet them again, and receive some further direction; but none came to his relief.—PP 147, 148.

All day he had hopes of meeting an angel coming to bless and comfort him, or perhaps to revoke the command of God, but no messenger of mercy appeared. . . . The second long day comes to a close, another sleepless night is spent in humiliation and prayer, and the journey of the third day is commenced.—ST April 1, 1875.

At the appointed place they built the altar and laid the wood upon it. Then with trembling voice, Abraham unfolded to his son the divine message. It was with terror and amazement that Isaac learned his fate, but he offered no resistance. . . . He was a sharer in Abraham's faith, and he felt that he was honored in being called to give his life as an offering to God. . . .

And now the last words of love are spoken, the last tears are shed, the last embrace is given. The father lifts the knife to slay his son, when suddenly his arm is stayed. An angel of God calls to the patriarch out of heaven, "Abraham, Abraham!" He quickly answers, "Here am I." And again the voice is heard, "Lay not thine hand upon the lad, neither do thou anything unto him; for now I know that thou fearest God, seeing thou hast not withheld thy son, thine only son, from me.". . .

God gave His Son to a death of agony and shame. The angels who witnessed the humiliation and soul anguish of the Son of God were not permitted to interpose, as in the case of Isaac. There was no voice to cry,

"It is enough." To save the fallen race, the King of glory yielded up His life. . . .

Heavenly beings were witnesses of the scene as the faith of Abraham and the submission of Isaac were tested. . . . All heaven beheld with wonder and admiration Abraham's unfaltering obedience. All heaven applauded his fidelity. Satan's accusations were shown to be false. . . .

It had been difficult even for the angels to grasp the mystery of redemption—to comprehend that the Commander of heaven, the Son of God, must die for guilty man. When the command was given to Abraham to offer up his son, the interest of all heavenly beings was enlisted. With intense earnestness they watched each step in the fulfillment of this command. When to Isaac's question, "Where is the lamb for a burnt offering?" Abraham made answer, "God will provide himself a lamb"; and when the father's hand was stayed as he was about to slay his son, and the ram which God had provided was offered in the place of Isaac—then light was shed upon the mystery of redemption, and even the angels understood more clearly the wonderful provision that God had made for man's salvation.—PP 152, 154, 155.

The Marriage of Isaac

In the mind of Abraham, the choice of a wife for his son [Isaac] was a matter of grave importance; he was anxious to have him marry one who would not lead him from God. . . .

Isaac, trusting to his father's wisdom and affection, was satisfied to commit the matter to him, believing also that God Himself would direct in the choice made. The patriarch's thoughts turned to his father's kindred in the land of Mesopotamia. . . . [He] committed the important matter to "his eldest servant [Eliezar]," a man of piety, experience, and sound judgment, who had rendered him long and faithful service. . . . "The Lord God of heaven," he said, "which took me from my father's house, and from the land of my kindred, . . . He shall send His angel before thee." . . . .

The messenger set out without delay. . . . [At] Haran, "the city of Nahor," he halted outside the walls, near the well to which the women of the place came at evening for water. . . . Remembering the words of Abraham, that God would send His angel with him, he prayed earnestly for positive guidance. In the family of his master he was accustomed to the constant exercise of kindness and hospitality, and he now asked that an act of courtesy might indicate the maiden whom God had chosen.

Hardly had the prayer been uttered before the answer was given. Among the women who were gathered at the well, the courteous manners of one [Rebekah] attracted his attention. As she came from the well, the stranger went to meet her, asking for some water from the pitcher upon her shoulder. The request received a kindly answer, with an offer to draw water for the camels also, a service which it was customary even for the daughters of princes to perform for their fathers' flocks and herds. Thus the desired sign was given. . . .

Abraham dwelt at Beersheba, and Isaac, who had been attending to the flocks in the adjoining country, had returned to his father's tent to await the arrival of the messenger from Haran. . . . "And Isaac went out to meditate in the field at the eventide. . . . And the servant told Isaac all the things that he had done. And Isaac brought her into his mother Sarah's tent, and took Rebekah, and she became his wife." —PP 171-173.

Jacob and Esau

Jacob and Esau, the twin sons of Isaac, present a striking contrast, both in character and life. This unlikeness was foretold by the angel of God before their birth. When in answer to Rebekah's troubled prayer he declared that two sons would be given her, he opened to her their future history, that each would become the head of a mighty nation, but that one would be greater than the other, and that the younger would have the preeminence. . . .

Isaac . . . plainly stated that Esau, as the eldest, was the one entitled to the birthright. But Esau had no love for devotion, no inclination to a religious life. . . . Rebekah remembered the words of the angel, and . . . she was convinced that the heritage of divine promise was intended for Jacob. She repeated to Isaac the angel's words; but the father's affections were centered upon the elder son, and he was unshaken in his purpose.—PP 177, 178.

Jacob had learned from his mother of the divine intimation that the birthright should fall to him, and he was filled with an unspeakable desire for the privileges which it would confer. It was not the possession of his father's wealth that he craved; the spiritual birthright was the object of his longing. . . .

When Esau, coming home one day faint and weary from the chase, asked for the food that Jacob was preparing, the latter . . . offered to satisfy his brother's hunger at the price of the birthright. "Behold, I am at the point to die," cried the reckless, self-indulgent hunter, "and what profit shall this birthright do to me?" And for a dish of red pottage he parted with his birthright. . . .

Jacob and Rebekah succeeded in their purpose, but they gained only trouble and sorrow by their deception. God had declared that Jacob should receive the birthright, and His word would have been fulfilled in His own time, had they waited in faith for Him to work for them. . . .

Threatened with death by the wrath of Esau, Jacob went out from his father's home a fugitive. . . . The evening of the second day found him far away from his father's tents. He felt that he was an outcast, and he knew that all this trouble had been brought upon him by his own wrong course. The darkness of despair pressed upon his soul, and he hardly dared to pray. But he was so utterly lonely that he felt the need of protection from God as he had never felt it before. With weeping and deep humiliation he confessed his sin, and entreated for some evidence that he was not utterly forsaken. . . .

God did not forsake Jacob. . . . The Lord compassionately revealed just what Jacob needed—a Saviour. . . . Wearied with his journey, the wanderer lay down upon the ground, with a stone for his pillow. As he slept, he beheld a ladder, bright and shining, whose base rested upon the earth, while the top reached to heaven. Upon this ladder, angels were ascending and descending; above it was the Lord of glory, and from the heavens His voice was heard: "I am the Lord God of Abraham thy father, and the God of Isaac.". . . .

In this vision the plan of redemption was presented to Jacob. . . . The ladder represents Jesus, the appointed medium of communication. Had He not with His own merits bridged the gulf that sin had made, the ministering angels could have held no communion with fallen man. . . .

With a new and abiding faith in the divine promises, and assured of the presence and guardianship of heavenly angels, Jacob pursued his journey to "the land of the children of the East."—PP 178-180, 183, 184, 188.

Though Jacob had left Padan-aram in obedience to the divine direction, it was not without many misgivings that he retraced the road which he had trodden as a fugitive twenty years before. His sin in the deception of his father was ever before him. . . . As he drew nearer his journey's end, the thought of Esau brought many a troubled foreboding. . . . Again the Lord granted Jacob a token of the divine care.—PP 195.

As Jacob went on his way, the angels of God met him. And when he saw them, he said, "This is God's host." He saw the angels of God in a dream, encamping around about him.—3SG 127.

Directly before . . . [Jacob], as if leading the way, he beheld two armies of heavenly angels marching as a guide and guard; and when he saw them he broke forth in language of praise, and exclaimed, "This is God's host." And he called the name of the place Mahanaim, which signifies two hosts, or camps.—ST Nov. 20, 1879.

Yet Jacob felt that he had something to do to secure his own safety. He therefore dispatched messengers with a conciliatory greeting to his brother. . . . But the servants returned with the tidings that Esau was approaching with four hundred men, and no response was sent to the friendly message. . . . "Jacob was greatly afraid and distressed." . . . He accordingly divided them [his family and servants] into two bands, so that if one should be attacked, the other might have an opportunity to escape. . . .

They had now reached the river Jabbok, and as night came on, Jacob sent his family across the ford of the river, while he alone remained behind. He had decided to spend the night in prayer, and he desired to be alone with God. . . .

Suddenly a strong hand was laid upon him. He thought that an enemy was seeking his life, and he endeavored to wrest himself from the grasp of his assailant. In the darkness the two struggled for the mastery. Not a word was spoken, but Jacob put forth all his strength, and did not relax his efforts for a moment. While he was thus battling for his life, the sense of his guilt pressed upon his soul; his sins rose up before him, to shut him out from God. But in his terrible extremity he remembered God's promises, and his whole heart went out in entreaty for His mercy. The struggle continued until near the break of day, when the stranger placed his finger upon Jacob's thigh, and he was crippled instantly. The patriarch now discerned the character of his antagonist. He knew that he had been in conflict with a heavenly messenger, and this was why his almost superhuman effort had not gained the victory.—PP 196, 197.

The One who wrestled with Jacob is called a man; Hosea calls Him the angel; while Jacob said, "I have seen God face to face." He is also said to have had power with God. It was the Majesty of heaven, the Angel of the covenant, that came, in the form and appearance of a man, to Jacob.—ST Nov. 20, 1879.

It was Christ, "the Angel of the covenant," who had revealed Himself to Jacob. The patriarch was now disabled, and suffering the keenest pain, but he would not loosen his hold. . . . He must have the assurance that his sin was pardoned. . . . The Angel tried to release Himself; He urged, "Let me go, for the day breaketh"; but Jacob answered, "I will not let thee go, except thou bless me." Had this been a boastful, presumptuous confidence, Jacob would have been instantly destroyed; but his was the assurance of one who confesses his own unworthiness, yet trusts the faithfulness of a covenant-keeping God. Jacob "had power over the Angel, and prevailed." . . .

While Jacob was wrestling with the Angel, another heavenly messenger was sent to Esau. In a dream, Esau beheld his brother for twenty years an exile from his father's house; he witnessed his grief at finding his mother dead; and saw him encompassed by the hosts of God. This dream was related by Esau to his soldiers, with the charge not to harm Jacob, for the God of his father was with him. . . .

Jacob's experience during that night of wrestling and anguish represents the trial through which the people of God must pass just before Christ's second coming. —PP 197-201.

8.

Angels at the Time of the Exodus

The Birth of Moses

As time rolled on, [Joseph] the great man to whom Egypt owed so much. . . passed to the grave. And "there arose up a new king over Egypt, which knew not Joseph." . . . . "And he said unto his people, Behold, the people of the children of Israel are more and mightier than we." . . . . Orders were issued. . . to destroy the Hebrew male children at their birth. Satan was the mover in this matter. He knew that a deliverer was to be raised up among the Israelites; and by leading the king to destroy their children he hoped to defeat the divine purpose. . . .

While this decree was in full force, a son was born to Amram and Jochebed. . . . The mother succeeded in concealing the child [Moses] for three months. Then, finding that she could no longer keep him safely, she prepared a little ark of rushes, making it watertight by means of slime and pitch; and laying the babe therein, she placed it among the flags at the river's brink. She dared not remain to guard it, lest the child's life and her own should be forfeited; but his sister, Miriam, lingered near, . . . anxiously watching to see what would become of her little brother. And there were other watchers. The mother's earnest prayers had committed her child to the care of God; and angels, unseen, hovered above his lowly resting place. Angels directed Pharaoh's daughter thither. Her curiosity was excited by the little basket, and as she looked upon the beautiful child within, she read the story at a glance. The tears of the babe awakened her compassion, and . . . she determined that he should be saved; she would adopt him as her own.—PP 241-243.

The elders of Israel were taught by angels that the time for their deliverance was near, and that Moses was the man whom God would employ to accomplish this work. Angels instructed Moses also that Jehovah had chosen him to break the bondage of his people. He, supposing that they were to obtain their freedom by force of arms, expected to lead the Hebrew host against the armies of Egypt.—PP 245.

Moses remained at court until he was forty years of age. . . . One day while thus abroad, seeing an Egyptian smiting an Israelite, he sprung forward, and slew the Egyptian . . . and immediately buried the body in the sand. . . . [Moses] made his escape and fled toward Arabia. . . . After a time, Moses married one of the daughters of Jethro; and here, in the service of his father-in-law, as keeper of his flocks, he remained forty years.—PP 246, 247.

Moses in Midian

Could his [Moses'] eyes have been opened, he would have seen the messengers of God, pure, holy angels, bending lovingly over him, shedding their light around him.—ST Feb. 19, 1880.

While engaged in his round of duties he [Moses] saw a bush, branches, foliage, and trunk, all burning, yet not consumed. He drew near to view the wonderful sight, when a voice addressed him from out of the flame. It was the voice of God. It was He who, as the angel of the covenant, had revealed Himself to the fathers in ages past. The frame of Moses quivered, he was thrilled with terror as the Lord called him by name. With trembling lips he answered, "Here am I." He was warned not to approach his Creator with undue familiarity: "Put off thy shoes from off thy feet; for the place whereon thou standest is holy ground." "And Moses hid his face; for he was afraid to look upon God."—ST Feb. 26, 1880.

With his wife and children, Moses set forth on the journey [to Egypt]. . . . On the way from Midian, Moses received a startling and terrible warning of the Lord's displeasure. An angel appeared to him in a threatening manner, as if he would immediately destroy him. No explanation was given; but Moses remembered that he had disregarded one of God's requirements; yielding to the persuasion of his wife, he had neglected to perform the rite of circumcision upon their youngest son. He had failed to comply with the condition by which his child could be entitled to the blessings of God's covenant with Israel. . . . Zipporah, fearing that her husband would be slain, performed the rite herself, and the angel then permitted Moses to pursue his journey. In his mission to Pharaoh, Moses was to be placed in a position of great peril; his life could be preserved only through the protection of holy angels. But while living in neglect of a known duty, he would not be secure; for he could not be shielded by the angels of God.—PP 255, 256.

Aaron, being instructed by angels, went forth to meet his brother, from whom he had been so long separated; and they met amid the desert solitudes, near Horeb. . . . Together they journeyed to Egypt; and having reached the land of Goshen, they proceeded to assemble the elders of Israel.—PP 257.

The Plagues of Egypt

Moses and Aaron were God's representatives to a bold, defiant king, and to impenitent priests, hardened in rebellion, who had allied themselves to evil angels. Pharaoh and the great men of Egypt were not ignorant in regard to the wise government of God. A bright light had been shining through the ages, pointing to God, to His righteous government, and to the claims of His law. Joseph and the children of Israel in Egypt had made known the knowledge of God. Even after the people of Israel had been brought into bondage to the Egyptians, not all were regarded as slaves. Many were placed in important positions, and these were witnesses for God.—YI April 8, 1897.

Satan . . . well knew that Moses was chosen of God to break the yoke of bondage upon the children of Israel. . . . He consulted with his angels how to accomplish a work which should answer a twofold purpose: 1. To destroy the influence of the work wrought by God through His servant Moses, by working through his agents, and thus counterfeiting the true work of God; 2. To exert an influence by his work through the magicians which would reach down through all ages and destroy in the minds of many true faith in the mighty miracles and works to be performed by Christ when He should come to this world.—1T 291.

Moses and Aaron entered the lordly halls of the king of Egypt. There, . . . before the monarch of the most powerful kingdom then in existence, stood the two representatives of the enslaved race, to repeat the command from God for Israel's release. The king demanded a miracle, in evidence of their divine commission. . . . Aaron now took the rod, and cast it down before Pharaoh. It became a serpent. The monarch sent for his "wise men and the sorcerers," who "cast down every man his rod, and they became serpents; but Aaron's rod swallowed up their rods." . . .

The magicians did not really cause their rods to become serpents; but by magic, aided by the great deceiver, they were able to produce this appearance. It was beyond the power of Satan to change the rods to living serpents. The prince of evil, though possessing all the wisdom and might of an angel fallen, has not power to create, or to give life; this is the prerogative of God alone. But all that was in Satan's power to do, he did; he produced a counterfeit. To human sight the rods were changed to serpents. . . . There was nothing in their appearance to distinguish them from the serpent produced by Moses. Though the Lord caused the real serpent to swallow up the spurious ones, yet even this was regarded by Pharaoh, not as a work of God's power, but as the result of a kind of magic superior to that of his servants.

Pharaoh desired to justify his stubbornness in resisting the divine command, and hence he was seeking some pretext for disregarding the miracles that God had wrought through Moses. Satan gave him just what he wanted. By the work that he wrought through the magicians, he made it appear to the Egyptians that Moses and Aaron were only magicians and sorcerers, and that the message they brought could not claim respect as coming from a superior being. Thus Satan's counterfeit accomplished its purpose, of emboldening the Egyptians in their rebellion, and causing Pharaoh to harden his heart against conviction. Satan hoped also to shake the faith of Moses and Aaron in the divine origin of their mission.—PP 263, 264.

When the miracles were wrought before the king, Satan was on the ground to counteract their influence and prevent Pharaoh from acknowledging the supremacy of God and obeying his mandate. Satan wrought to the utmost of his power to counterfeit the work of God and resist His will. The only result was to prepare the way for greater exhibitions of the divine power and glory, and to make more apparent, both to the Israelites and to all Egypt, the existence and sovereignty of the true and living God.—PP 334.

The storm [the seventh plague] came on the morrow as predicted—thunder and hail, and fire mingled with it, destroying every herb, shattering trees, and smiting man and beast. Hitherto none of the lives of the Egyptians had been taken, but now death and desolation followed in the track of the destroying angel. The land of Goshen alone was spared.—ST March 18, 1880.

The Lord through Moses gave direction to the children of Israel concerning their departure from Egypt, and especially for their preservation from the coming judgment. Each family, alone or in connection with others, was to slay a lamb or a kid "without blemish," and with a bunch of hyssop sprinkle its blood on "the two sideposts and on the upper doorpost" of the house, that the destroying angel, coming at midnight, might not enter that dwelling. . . .

The Lord declared: "I will pass through the land of Egypt this night, and will smite all the first-born in the land. . . . And the blood shall be to you for a token upon the houses where ye are; and when I see the blood, I will pass over you, and the plague shall not be upon you to destroy you."—PP 274.

The children of Israel had followed the directions given them of God; and while the angel of death was passing from house to house among the Egyptians, they were all ready for their journey.—1SP 204.

About midnight every Egyptian household was aroused from their sleep by the cry of pain. They feared they were all to die. They remembered when the cry of distress and mourning was heard from the Hebrews because of the inhuman decree of a cruel king to slay all their male infants as soon as they were born. The Egyptians could not see the avenging angel, who entered every house and dealt the death blow, but they knew that it was the Hebrews' God who was causing them to suffer the same distress they had made the Israelites to suffer.—YI May 1, 1873.

Christ, Israel's Invisible Leader

In Egypt the report was spread that the children of Israel . . . were pressing on toward the Red Sea. . . . Pharaoh collected his forces . . . [and] attended by the great men of his realm, headed the attacking army.

The Hebrews were encamped beside the sea. . . . Suddenly they beheld in the distance the flashing armor and moving chariots betokening the advance guard of a great army. . . . Terror filled the hearts of Israel. Some cried unto the Lord, but the far greater part hastened to Moses with their complaints. . . . His calm and assuring reply to the people was, "Fear ye not, stand still, and see the salvation of the Lord." . . .

The wonderful pillar of cloud had been followed as the signal of God to go forward; but now they questioned among themselves if it might not foreshadow some great calamity; for had it not led them on the wrong side of the mountain, into an impassable way? Thus the angel of God appeared to their deluded minds as the harbinger of disaster.

But now, as the Egyptian host approached them, expecting to make them an easy prey, the cloudy column rose majestically into the heavens, passed over the Israelites, and descended between them and the armies of Egypt. A wall of darkness interposed between the pursued and their pursuers. The Egyptians could no longer discern the camp of the Hebrews, and were forced to halt. But as the darkness of night deepened, the wall of cloud became a great light to the Hebrews, flooding the entire encampment with the radiance of day.

Then hope returned to the hearts of Israel. And Moses lifted up his voice unto the Lord. "And the Lord said unto Moses, . . . Speak unto the children of Israel, that they go forward. But lift thou up thy rod, and stretch out thine hand over the sea, and divide it: and the children of Israel shall go on dry ground through the midst of the sea." . . .

"The Egyptians pursued, and went in after them to the midst of the sea, even all Pharaoh's horses, his chariots, and his horsemen. And it came to pass, that in the morning watch the Lord looked unto the host of the Egyptians through the pillar of fire and of the cloud, and troubled the host of the Egyptians."—PP 283-287.

Angels of God went through their host and removed their chariot wheels.—1SP 209.

The Egyptians were seized with confusion and dismay. . . , they endeavored to retrace their steps, and flee to the shore they had quitted. But Moses stretched out his rod, and the piled-up waters, hissing, roaring, and eager for their prey, rushed together, and swallowed the Egyptian army in their black depths.—PP 287.

[The] Leader [of the Israelites] was a mighty general of armies. His angels, that do His bidding, walked on either side of the vast armies of Israel, and no harm could come to them. Israel was safe. . . . Then came the sacred song of triumph, led by Miriam.—RH June 1, 1897.

Jesus was the angel enshrouded in the pillar of cloud by day and the pillar of fire by night.—RH June 17, 1890.

9.

Angels From Sinai to the Taking of Jericho

Angels in Israel's Wilderness Wanderings

Christ was the angel appointed of God to go before Moses in the wilderness, conducting the Israelites in their travels to the land of Canaan.—RH May 6, 1875.

In all the way of God's leading, they [the Israelites] had found water to refresh the thirsty, bread from heaven to satisfy their hunger, and peace and safety under the shadowy cloud by day and the fiery pillar by night. Angels were ministering to them as they climbed the rocky heights, or threaded the rugged paths of the wilderness.—ST Oct. 21, 1880.

God manifested His great care and love for His people in sending them bread from heaven. "Man did eat angels' food"; that is, food provided for them by the angels.—1SP 226.

Israel at Sinai

And now before them in solemn majesty Mount Sinai

lifted its massive front. The cloudy pillar rested upon its summit, and the people spread their tents upon the plain beneath. Here was to be their home for nearly a year. At night the pillar of fire assured them of the divine protection, and while they were locked in slumber, the bread of heaven fell gently upon the encampment. . . .

Soon after the encampment at Sinai, Moses was called up into the mountain to meet with God. Alone he climbed the steep and rugged path, and drew near to the cloud that marked the place of Jehovah's presence. Israel was now to be taken into a close and peculiar relation to the Most High. . . .

Speaking out of the thick darkness that enshrouded Him, as He stood upon the mount, surrounded by a retinue of angels, the Lord made known His law. . . . Arrangements were now to be made for the full establishment of the chosen nation under Jehovah as their king.—PP 301, 303, 304, 312.

"Let Them Make Me a Sanctuary"

During his stay in the mount, Moses received directions for the building of a sanctuary in which the divine presence would be specially manifested. "Let them make me a sanctuary, that I may dwell among them," was the command of God.—PP 313.

The building [tabernacle] was divided into two apartments by a rich and beautiful curtain, or veil, suspended from gold-plated pillars; and a similar veil closed the entrance of the first apartment. These, like the inner covering, which formed the ceiling, were of the most gorgeous colors, blue, purple, and scarlet, beautifully arranged, while inwrought with threads of gold and silver were cherubim to represent the angelic host who are connected with the work of the heavenly sanctuary, and who are ministering spirits to the people of God on earth.—PP 347.

After the building of the tabernacle was completed, Moses examined all the work, and compared it with the pattern, and directions he had received of God, and he saw that every part of it agreed with the pattern; and he blessed the people. God gave a pattern of the ark to Moses, with special directions how to make it. The ark was made to contain the tables of stone, on which God engraved, with His own finger, the ten commandments. It was in form like a chest, and was overlaid and inlaid with pure gold. It was ornamented with crowns of gold round about the top.

The cover of this sacred chest was the mercy-seat, made of solid gold. On each end of the mercy-seat was fixed a cherub of pure, solid gold. Their faces were turned toward each other, and were looking reverentially downward toward the mercy-seat, which represents all the heavenly angels looking with interest and reverence to the law of God deposited in the ark in the heavenly sanctuary. These cherubs had wings. One wing of each angel was stretched forth on high, while the other wing of each angel covered their forms.

The ark of the earthly sanctuary was the pattern of the true ark in heaven. There, beside the heavenly ark, stand living angels, at either end of the ark, each with one wing overshadowing the mercy-seat, and stretching forth on high, while the other wings are folded over their forms in token of reverence and humility.—1SP 272.

Above the mercy-seat was the shekinah, the manifestation of the divine presence; and from between the cherubim, God made known His will. Divine messages were sometimes communicated to the high priest by a voice from the cloud.—PP 349.

When the Lord did not answer by a voice, He let the sacred beams of light and glory rest upon the cherubim upon the right of the ark, in approbation, or favor. If their requests were refused, a cloud rested upon the cherubim at the left.—1SP 399.

Through Christ was to be fulfilled the purpose of which the tabernacle was a symbol—that glorious building, its walls of glistening gold reflecting in rainbow hues the curtains inwrought with cherubim, the fragrance of ever-burning incense pervading all, the priests robed in spotless white, and in the deep mystery of the inner place, above the mercy-seat, between the figures of the bowed, worshiping angels, the glory of the Holiest. In all, God desired His people to read His purpose for the human soul. It was the same purpose long afterward set forth by the apostle Paul, speaking by the Holy Spirit:

"Know ye not that ye are the temple of God, and that the Spirit of God dwelleth in you?"—Ed 36.

At the very foot of Sinai, Satan began to execute his plans for overthrowing the law of God, thus carrying forward the same work he had begun in heaven. During the forty days while Moses was in the mount with God, Satan was busy, exciting doubt, apostasy, and rebellion. While God was writing down His law, to be committed to His covenant people, the Israelites, denying their loyalty to Jehovah, were demanding gods of gold! . . .

The whole universe had been witness to the scenes at Sinai. In the working out of the two administrations was seen the contrast between the government of God and that of Satan. Again the sinless inhabitants of other worlds beheld the results of Satan's apostasy, and the kind of government he would have established in heaven, had he been permitted to bear sway.—PP 335, 336.

Can we marvel that the "excellent glory" reflected from Omnipotence shone in Moses' face with such brightness that the people could not look upon it? The impress of God was upon him, making him appear as one of the shining angels from the throne.—4T 533.

Throughout their journeyings, as they [the Israelites] complained of the difficulties in the way, and murmured against their leaders, Moses had told them, "Your murmurings are against God. It is not I, but God, who has wrought in your deliverance." But his hasty words before the rock, "Shall *we* bring water?" were a virtual admission of their charge. . . . The Lord would remove this impression forever from their minds, by forbidding Moses to enter the Promised Land. Here was unmistakable evidence that their leader was not Moses, but the mighty Angel of whom the Lord had said, "Behold, I send an Angel before thee, to keep thee in the way, and to bring thee into the place which I have prepared. Beware of him, and obey his voice; . . . for my name is in him."—PP 419.

The Death and Resurrection of Moses

Moses turned from the congregation, and in silence and alone made his way up the mountainside. . . . Upon that lonely height he stood, and gazed with undimmed eye upon the scene spread out before him.—PP 471.

It was not the will of God that anyone should go up with Moses to the top of Pisgah. There he stood, upon a high prominence upon Pisgah's top, in the presence of God and heavenly angels.—4aSG 57.

The angels also revealed to Moses that although he mourned because he had sinned and could not enter the Promised Land, and although he felt that he had caused the children of Israel to sin, yet it was their own sin, their murmuring and complaining spirit, that had led him to deviate from the right and commit a sin that kept him out of the Promised Land. The angels told him that he was not the greatest sufferer, that he did not feel in his heart the fullest depth of their sin, but that Christ, their invisible leader, was the one against whom they had transgressed. . . .

The heavenly messengers also referred to the sacrificial offerings typifying the crucifixion of Christ, and opened before Moses' mind the events that should take place in the future. . . . When the view of the crucifixion was presented before Moses, what a scene there must have been on Pisgah's summit! . . . He viewed the panoramic scenes passing before him in which he saw the sufferings of the Angel who had led the Israelites through the wilderness, guiding them in their wandering journey from Egypt to Canaan. . . . When he beheld the Saviour's ascension and saw that he himself would be one of those who should attend the Saviour and open to Him the everlasting gates, what a change took place in the expression on his face! . . .

He saw the earth purified by fire and cleansed from every vestige of sin, every mark of the curse, and renovated and given to the saints to possess forever and ever. . . . As Moses beheld this scene, joy and triumph were expressed in his countenance. He could understand the force of all the angels revealed to him. He took in the whole scene as it was presented before him.—10MR 151, 152, 154, 155, 158, 159.

After he had viewed Canaan to his satisfaction, he lay down like a tired warrior, to rest. Sleep came upon him, but it was the sleep of death. Angels took his body and buried it in the valley. The Israelites could never find the place where he was buried. . . .

Satan exulted that he had succeeded in causing Moses to sin against God. For this transgression, Moses came under the dominion of death. If he had continued faithful, and his life had not been marred with that one transgression, in failing to give to God the glory of bringing water from the rock, he would have entered the Promised Land, and would have been translated to heaven without seeing death. Michael, or Christ, with the angels that buried Moses, came down from heaven, after he had remained in the grave a short time, and resurrected him.—4aSG 57, 58.

The power of the grave had never been broken, and all who were in the tomb he [Satan] claimed as his captives, never to be released from his dark prison-house.

For the first time, Christ was about to give life to the dead. As the Prince of life and the shining ones approached the grave, Satan was alarmed for his supremacy. With his evil angels he stood to dispute an invasion of the territory that he claimed as his own. —PP 478.

As Christ and the angels approached the grave, Satan and his angels appeared at the grave, and were guarding the body of Moses, lest it should be removed. As Christ and His angels drew nigh, Satan resisted their approach, but was compelled by the glory and power of Christ and His angels to fall back. Satan claimed the body of Moses, because of his one transgression; but Christ meekly referred him to His Father, saying, "The Lord rebuke thee." Christ told Satan that He knew that Moses had humbly repented of this one wrong, and no stain rested upon his character, and his name in the heavenly book of records stood untarnished. Then Christ resurrected the body of Moses.—4aSG 58.

Balaam, a Prophet Gone Wrong

God came to Balaam in the night, through one of His angels, and inquired of him, What men are these with thee? And Balaam said unto God, Balak the "son of Zippor, king of Moab, hath sent unto me, saying, Behold, there is a people come out of Egypt. . . . Come, now, curse me them. . . . And God said unto Balaam, Thou shalt not go with them. Thou shalt not curse the people; for they are blessed." The angel tells Balaam that the children of Israel are conducted under the banner of the God of heaven; and no curse from man could retard their progress.

In the morning he [Balaam] arose, and reluctantly told the men to return to Balak, for the Lord would not suffer him to go with them. Then Balak sent other princes, . . . occupying a more exalted position than the former messengers; and this time Balak's call was more urgent. "Let nothing, I pray thee, hinder thee coming unto me, for I will promote thee unto very great honor. . . . And Balaam answered and said, . . . If Balak would give me his house full of silver and gold, I cannot go beyond the word of the Lord my God, to do less or more."—4aSG 44.

A second time Balaam was tested. . . . He longed to comply with the king's request; and although the will of God had already been definitely made known to him, he urged the messengers to tarry, that he might further inquire of God; as though the Infinite One were a man, to be persuaded.—PP 440.

An angel was sent to Balaam to say unto him, "If the men come to call thee, rise up, and go with them; but yet the word which I shall say unto thee, that shalt thou do."—1SP 321.

Balaam had received permission to go with the messengers from Moab, if they came in the morning to call him. But annoyed at his delay, and expecting another refusal, they set out on their homeward journey without further consultation with him. Every excuse for complying with the request of Balak had now been removed. But Balaam was determined to secure the reward; and taking the beast upon which he was accustomed to ride, he set out on the journey. He feared that even now the divine permission might be withdrawn, and he pressed eagerly forward, impatient lest he should by some means fail to gain the coveted reward.—PP 441.

God's anger was kindled against Balaam for his Heaven-daring folly, and "an angel of the Lord stood in the way for an adversary against him." The animal, seeing the divine messenger, who was, however, invisible to the master, turned aside from the highway into a field. With cruel blows, Balaam brought the beast back into the path; but again, in a narrow place hemmed in by walls, the angel appeared, and the animal, trying to avoid the menacing figure, crushed the rider's foot against the wall.—ST Nov. 25, 1880.

Balaam's rage was unbounded, and with his staff he smote the animal more cruelly than before. God now opened its mouth, and by "the dumb ass speaking with man's voice," He "forbade the madness of the prophet." 2 Peter 2:16. "What have I done unto thee," it said, "that thou hast smitten me these three times?"

Furious at being thus hindered in his journey, Balaam answered the beast as he would have addressed an intelligent being—"Because thou hast mocked me: I would there were a sword in mine hand, for now would I kill thee." . . .

The eyes of Balaam were now opened, and he beheld the angel of God standing with drawn sword ready to slay him. In terror "he bowed down his head, and fell flat on his face." The angel said to him, "Wherefore hast thou smitten thine ass these three times? Behold, I went out to withstand thee, because thy way is perverse before me: and the ass saw me, and turned from me these three times: unless she had turned from me, surely now also I had slain thee." . . .

When he beheld the messenger of God, Balaam exclaimed in terror, "I have sinned; for I knew not that thou stoodest in the way against me: now therefore, if it displease thee, I will get me back again."—PP 442, 443.

After the angel had impressively warned Balaam against gratifying the Moabites, he gave him permission to pursue his journey. . . .

Balak met Balaam, and inquired of him why he thus delayed to come when he sent for him; . . . Balaam answered, Lo, I am come unto thee. He then told him that he had no power to say anything. The word that God should give him, that could he speak, and could go no further. Balaam ordered the sacrifices according to the religious rites. God sent His angel to meet with Balaam, to give him words of utterance, as He had done on occasions when Balaam was wholly devoted to the service of God. "And the Lord put a word in Balaam's mouth, and . . . he took up his parable, and said, Balak, the king of Moab, hath brought me from Aram, . . . saying,

Come, curse me Jacob, and come, defy Israel. How shall I curse, whom God hath not cursed? or how shall I defy, whom the Lord hath not defied?". . .

Balak was disappointed and angry. He exclaims, "What hast thou done unto me? I took thee to curse mine enemies, and, behold, thou hast blessed them altogether." Balak thinks it is the grand appearance of the Israelites in their tents . . . that keeps him from cursing them. He thinks if he takes him to . . . where Israel will not appear to such advantage, he can obtain a curse from Balaam. Again, at Zophim . . . Balaam offered burnt offerings, and then went by himself to commune with the angel of God. And the angel told Balaam what to say.—1SP 322-324.

Joshua Leads Israel Into Canaan

The Israelites deeply mourned for [Moses] their departed leader, and thirty days were devoted to special services in honor of his memory. . . . Joshua was now the acknowledged leader of Israel. . . .

Orders were now issued to make ready for an advance. . . . Leaving their encampment . . . the host descended to the border of the Jordan.—PP 481, 483.

Four heavenly angels always accompanied the ark of God in all its journeyings, to guard it from all danger, and to fulfill any mission required of them in connection with the ark. Jesus the Son of God, followed by heavenly angels, went before the ark as it came to Jordan; and the waters were cut off before His presence. Christ and angels stood by the ark and the priests in the bed of the river, until all Israel had passed over Jordan.—1SP 399.

If the eyes of Joshua had been opened . . . and he could have endured the sight, he would have seen the angels of the Lord encamped about the children of Israel; for the trained army of heaven had come to fight for the people of God, and the Captain of the Lord's host was there to command.—RH July 19, 1892.

As Joshua withdrew from the armies of Israel, to meditate and pray for God's special presence to attend him, he saw a man of lofty stature, clad in warlike garments, with his sword in his hand. . . . This was no common angel. It was the Lord Jesus Christ, He who had conducted the Hebrews through the wilderness, enshrouded in the pillar of fire by night, and a pillar of cloud by day. The place was made sacred by His presence, therefore Joshua was commanded to put off his shoes.—4aSG 61.

Awe-stricken, Joshua fell upon his face and worshiped, and heard the assurance, "I have given into thine hand Jericho, and the king thereof, and the mighty men of valor," and he received instruction for the capture of the city.—PP 488.

The Captain of the Lord's host did not reveal Himself to all the congregation. He communicated only with Joshua, who related the story of this interview to the Hebrews. It rested with them to believe or to doubt the words of Joshua, to follow the commands given by him in the name of the Captain of the Lord's host, or to rebel against his directions and deny his authority. *They could not see the host of angels, marshaled by the Son of God.*—4T 162, 163.

The Taking of Jericho

The Captain of the Lord's host Himself came from heaven to lead the armies of heaven in an attack upon the city. Angels of God laid hold of the massive walls and brought them to the ground.—3T 264.

Christ and angels attended the circuit of the ark around Jericho, and finally cast down the massive walls of the city, and delivered Jericho into the hands of Israel.—1SP 399.

When Jericho fell, no human hand touched the walls of the city, for the angels of the Lord overthrew the fortifications, and entered the fortress of the enemy. It was not Israel, but the Captain of the Lord's host that took Jericho. But Israel had their part to act to show their faith in the Captain of their salvation.—RH July 19, 1892.

If a single warrior had brought his strength to bear against the walls, the glory of God would have been lessened and His will frustrated. But the work was left to the Almighty; and had the foundation of the battlements been laid in the center of the earth and their summits reached the arch of heaven, the result would have been all the same, when the Captain of the Lord's host led His legions of angels to the attack.—ST April 14, 1881.

10.

Angels From the Time of the Judges to the Early Kingdom

Christ as the "Angel of the Lord"

When God sent His angels anciently to minister or communicate to individuals, when they learned that it was an angel they had seen and talked with, they were struck with awe, and were afraid that they should die. They had such exalted views of the terrible majesty and power of God, they thought to be brought into such close connection with one direct from His holy presence, would destroy them. . . . Judges 6:22, 23; 13:21, 22; Josh. 5, 13-15.—4bSG 152.

After the death of their leader [Joshua] and of the elders who were associated with him, the people began gradually to relapse into idolatry. . . .

The Lord did not permit the sins of His people to pass without rebuke. There were still faithful worshipers in Israel; and many others, from habit and early association, attended the worship of God at the tabernacle. A large company were assembled upon the occasion of a religious feast, when an angel of God, having first appeared at Gilgal, revealed himself to the congregation at Shiloh. . . .

This angel, the same that appeared to Joshua at the taking of Jericho, was no less a personage than the Son of God. . . . He showed them that He had not broken His promises to them, but they themselves had violated their solemn covenant.

"And it came to pass, when the angel of the Lord spake these words unto all the children of Israel, that the people lifted up their voice and wept." "And they sacrificed there unto the Lord." But their repentance produced no lasting results.—ST June 2, 1881.

Gideon

Gideon was the son of Joash, of the tribe of Manasseh. The division to which this family belonged held no leading position, but the household of Joash was distinguished for courage and integrity. . . . To Gideon came the divine call to deliver his people. He was engaged at the time in threshing wheat. . . . As Gideon labored in secrecy and silence, he sadly pondered upon the condition of Israel, and considered how the oppressor's yoke might be broken from off his people.

Suddenly the "Angel of the Lord" appeared and addressed him with the words, "Jehovah is with thee, thou mighty man of valor."—PP 546.

The angel had veiled the divine glory of His presence, but it was no other than Christ, the Son of God. When a prophet or an angel delivered a divine message, his words were, "The Lord saith, I will do this," but it is stated of the Person who talked with Gideon, "The Lord said unto him, I will be with thee."

Desiring to show special honor to his illustrious visitor, and having obtained the assurance that the Angel would tarry, Gideon hastened to his tent, and out of his scanty store prepared a kid and unleavened cakes, which he brought forth to set before Him. . . .

As the gift was presented, the Angel said, "Take the flesh and unleavened cakes, and lay them on this rock, and pour out the broth." Gideon did so, and then the Lord gave him the sign which he desired. With the staff in His hand, the Angel touched the flesh and the unleavened cakes, and a fire rose up out of the rock and consumed the whole as a sacrifice, and not as a hospitable meal; for He was God, and not man. After this token of His divine character, the Angel disappeared.

When convinced that he had looked upon the Son of God, Gideon was filled with fear, and exclaimed, "Alas, O Lord God! for because I have seen an Angel of the Lord face to face."

Then the Lord graciously appeared to Gideon a second time and said, "Peace be unto thee, fear not, thou shalt not die." These gracious words were spoken by the same compassionate Saviour who said to the tempted disciples upon the stormy sea, "It is I; be not afraid"—He who appeared to those sorrowing ones in the upper chamber, and spoke the selfsame words addressed to Gideon, "Peace be unto you."—ST June 23, 1881.

Samson

Amid the widespread apostasy, the faithful worshipers of God continued to plead with Him for the deliverance of Israel. . . . On the border of the hill country overlooking the Philistine plain, was the little town of Zorah. Here dwelt the family of Manoah, of the tribe of Dan, one of the few households that amid the general defection had remained true to Jehovah. To the childless wife of Manoah, "the Angel of Jehovah" appeared with the message that she should have a son, through whom God would begin to deliver Israel. In view of this, the Angel gave her instruction concerning her own habits, and also for the treatment of her child. . . .

The woman sought her husband, and, after describing the Angel, she repeated His message. Then, fearful that they should make some mistake in the important work committed to them, the husband prayed, "Let the man of God which thou didst send come again unto us, and teach us what we shall do unto the child that shall be born."

When the Angel again appeared, Manoah's anxious inquiry was, "How shall we order the child, and how shall we do unto him?" The previous instruction was repeated—"Of all that I said unto the woman let her beware. She may not eat of anything that cometh of the vine, neither let her drink wine or strong drink, nor eat any unclean thing. All that I commanded her let her observe."—PP 560, 561.

Manoah and his wife knew not that the One thus addressing them was Jesus Christ. They looked upon Him as the Lord's messenger, but whether a prophet or an angel, they were at a loss to determine. Wishing to manifest hospitality toward their guest, they entreated him to remain while they should prepare for Him a kid. But in their ignorance of His character, they knew not whether to offer it for a burnt offering or to place it before Him as food.

The angel answered, "Although thou detain me, I will not eat of thy bread; and if thou wilt offer a burnt offering, thou must offer it unto the Lord." Feeling assured, now, that his visitor was a prophet, Manoah said, "What is thy name, that when thy sayings come to pass we may do thee honor?"

The answer was, "Why askest thou after my name, seeing it is secret?" Perceiving the divine character of his guest, Manoah "took a kid, with a meat offering, and offered it upon a rock unto the Lord; and the angel did wondrously; and Manoah and his wife looked on." Fire came from the rock, and consumed the sacrifice, and as the flame went up toward heaven, "the angel of the Lord ascended in the flame of the altar. And Manoah and his wife looked on it, and fell on their faces to the ground." There could be no further question as to the character of their visitor. They knew that they had looked upon the Holy One, who, veiling His glory in the cloudy pillar, had been the guide and helper of Israel in the desert.

Amazement, awe, and terror filled Manoah's heart, and he could only exclaim, "We shall surely die, because we have seen God!" But his companion in that solemn hour possessed more faith than he. She reminded him that the Lord had been pleased to accept their sacrifice, and had promised them a son who should begin to deliver Israel. This was an evidence of favor instead of wrath.—ST Sept. 15, 1881.

The divine promise to Manoah was in due time fulfilled in the birth of a son, upon whom the name of Samson was bestowed. By the command of the angel no razor was to come upon the child's head, he being consecrated to God as a Nazarite, from his birth.—ST Oct. 6, 1881.

Samuel and Eli

Samuel was a child surrounded by the most corrupting influences. He saw and heard things that grieved his soul. The sons of Eli, who ministered in holy office, were controlled by Satan. These men polluted the whole atmosphere which surrounded them. Men and women were daily fascinated with sin and wrong, yet Samuel walked untainted. His robes of character were spotless. He did not fellowship, or have the least delight in, the sins which filled all Israel with fearful reports. Samuel loved God; he kept his soul in such close connection with heaven that an angel was sent to talk with him in reference to the sins of Eli's sons, which were corrupting Israel.—3T 472, 473.

The transgressions of Eli's sons were so daring, . . . that no sacrifice could atone for such willful transgression. . . . These sinners conducted the ark to the camp of Israel. . . .

God permitted His ark to be taken by their enemies to show Israel how vain it was to trust in the ark, the symbol of His presence, while they were profaning the commandments contained in the ark. . . .

The Philistines were triumphant, because they had, as they thought, the famous god of the Israelites, which had performed such wonders for them, and had made them a terror to their enemies. They took the ark of God to Ashdod, and set it in a splendid temple, made in honor of their most popular god, Dagon, and placed it by the side of their god. In the morning the priests of these gods entered the temple, and they were terrified to find Dagon fallen upon his face to the ground before the ark of the Lord. . . . The angels of God, who ever accompanied the ark, prostrated the senseless idol god, and afterward mutilated it, to show that God, the living God, was above all gods, and before Him every heathen god was as nothing.—4aSG 106, 107.

The men of Beth-shemesh quickly spread the tidings that the ark was in their possession, and the people from the surrounding country flocked to welcome its return. The ark had been placed upon the stone that first served for an altar, and before it additional sacrifices were offered unto the Lord. . . . Instead of preparing a suitable place for its reception, they permitted it to remain in the harvest field. As they continued to gaze upon the sacred chest and to talk of the wonderful manner in which it had been restored, they began to conjecture wherein lay its peculiar power. At last, overcome by curiosity, they removed the coverings and ventured to open it. . . .

Even the heathen Philistines had not dared to remove its coverings. Angels of heaven, unseen, ever attended it in all its journeyings. The irreverent daring of the people of Beth-shemesh was speedily punished. Many were smitten with sudden death.—PP 589.

Saul and Jonathan

God had raised up Samuel to judge Israel. He was honored by all the people. God was to be acknowledged as their great Head, yet He designated their rulers, and imbued them with His Spirit, and communicated His will to them through His angels.—4aSG 67.

Because of Saul's sin in his presumptuous offering, the Lord would not give him the honor of vanquishing the Philistines. Jonathan, the king's son, a man who feared the Lord, was chosen as the instrument to deliver Israel. . . .

Angels of heaven shielded Jonathan and his attendant, angels fought by their side, and the Philistines fell before them.—PP 623.

Angels of God fought by the side of Jonathan, and the Philistines fell all around him. Great fear seized the host of the Philistines in the field and in the garrison. . . . The earth trembled beneath them, as though a great multitude with horsemen and chariots were upon the ground prepared for battle. Jonathan and his armor-bearer, and even the Philistine host knew that the Lord was working for the deliverance of the Hebrews.—4aSG 70.

David's Early Years

Samuel came no more to Saul with directions from God. The Lord could not employ him to carry out His purposes. But He sent Samuel to the house of Jesse, to anoint David, whom He had selected to be ruler in place of Saul, whom He had rejected.

As the sons of Jesse passed before Samuel, he would have selected Eliab, who was of high stature, and dignified appearance, but the angel of God stood by him to guide him in the important decision, and instructed him that he should not judge from appearance. Eliab did not fear the Lord. His heart was not right with God. He would make a proud, exacting ruler. None were found among the sons of Jesse but David, the youngest, whose humble occupation was that of tending sheep.—4aSG 77, 78.

David was not of lofty stature; but his countenance was beautiful, expressive of humility, honesty, and true courage. The angel of God signified to Samuel that David was the one for him to anoint, for he was God's chosen. From that time the Lord gave David a prudent and understanding heart.—1SP 368.

David's eldest brother, Eliab, . . . was jealous of David, because he was honored before him. He despised David, and looked upon him as inferior to himself. He accused him before others of stealing away unknown to his father to see the battle. . . . David repels the unjust charge, and says, "What have I now done? Is there not a cause?" David is not careful to explain to his brother that he had come to the help of Israel; that God had sent him to slay Goliath. God had chosen him to be a ruler of Israel; and as the armies of the living God were in such peril, he had been directed by an angel to save Israel.—1SP 371.

Saul Encounters an Angel

[Saul] allowed his impulses to control his judgment, until he was plunged into a fury of passion. He had paroxysms of rage and madness, when he was ready to take the life of any that dared oppose his will. . . . It was David's blameless character and noble fidelity that had aroused the wrath of the king; and he deemed the very life and presence of David cast a reproach upon him. . . .

He came to Ramah, and halted at a great well in Sechu. The people were coming together to draw water, and he inquired where Samuel and David were staying. When he was told that they were at Naioth, he made haste to reach that place. But the angel of God met him on the way and controlled him. The Spirit of God held him in its power, and he went on his way uttering prayers to God, interspersed with predictions and sacred melodies. He prophesied of the coming of Messiah as the world's Redeemer. When he came to Naioth in Ramah, he laid aside his outer garments that betokened his station, and all day, and all night, he lay before Samuel and his pupils, under the influence of the divine Spirit.—ST Aug. 24, 1888.

Saul's Séance at Endor and His Death

Again war was declared between Israel and the Philistines. . . . Saul had learned that David and his force were with the Philistines, and he expected that the son of Jesse would take this opportunity to revenge the wrongs he had suffered. The king was in sore distress. . . . On the morrow, Saul must engage the Philistines in battle. The shadows of impending doom gathered dark about him; he longed for help and guidance. But it was in vain that he sought counsel from God. "The Lord answered him not, neither by dreams, nor by Urim, nor by prophets." . . .

Then said Saul unto his servants, "Seek me a woman that hath a familiar spirit, that I may go to her, and inquire of her." . . . It was told the king that a woman who had a familiar spirit was living in concealment at Endor. This woman had entered into covenant with Satan to yield herself to his control, to fulfill his purposes; and in return, the prince of evil wrought wonders for her, and revealed secret things to her.

Disguising himself, Saul went forth by night with but two attendants, to seek the retreat of the sorceress. . . . Under the cover of darkness, Saul and his attendants made their way across the plain, and safely passing the Philistine host, they crossed the mountain ridge, to the lonely home of the sorceress of Endor. . . .

After practicing her incantations, she said, "I saw gods ascending out of the earth. . . . An old man cometh up, and he is covered with a mantle. And Saul perceived that it was Samuel.". . .

It was not God's holy prophet that came forth at the spell of a sorcerer's incantation. Samuel was not present in that haunt of evil spirits. That supernatural appearance was produced solely by the power of Satan.—PP 675, 676, 679.

The woman's first words under the spell of her incantation had been addressed to the king, "Why hast thou deceived me? for thou art Saul." Thus the first act of the evil spirit which personated the prophet, was to communicate secretly with this wicked woman, to warn her of the deception that had been practiced upon her. The message to Saul from the pretended prophet was, "Why hast thou disquieted me, to bring me up? And Saul answered, I am sore distressed; for the Philistines make war against me, and God is departed from me, and answereth me no more, neither by prophets, nor by dreams; therefore I have called thee, that thou mayest make known unto me what I shall do."

When Samuel was living, Saul had despised his counsel, and had resented his reproofs. But now, in the hour of his distress and calamity, he felt that the prophet's guidance was his only hope, and in order to communicate with Heaven's ambassador, he vainly had recourse to the messenger of hell! Saul had placed himself fully in the power of Satan; and now he whose only delight is in causing misery and destruction, made the most of his advantage, to work the ruin of the unhappy king. In answer to Saul's agonized entreaty came the terrible message, professedly from the lips of Samuel:

"Wherefore then dost thou ask of me, seeing the Lord is departed from thee, and is become thine enemy? . . . Because thou obeyedst not the voice of the Lord, . . . therefore . . . the Lord will also deliver Israel with thee into the hand of the Philistines."—PP 680.

When Saul inquired for Samuel, the Lord did not cause Samuel to appear to Saul. He saw nothing. Satan was not allowed to disturb the rest of Samuel in the grave, and bring him up in reality to the witch of Endor. God does not give Satan power to resurrect the dead. But Satan's angels assume the form of dead friends, and speak and act like them, that through professed dead friends he can better carry on his work of deception. Satan knew Samuel well, and he knew how to represent him before the witch of Endor, and to utter correctly the fate of Saul and his sons.—1SP 376.

The Scripture account of Saul's visit to the woman of Endor has been a source of perplexity to many students of the Bible. There are some who take the position that Samuel was actually present at the interview with Saul, but the Bible itself furnishes sufficient ground for a contrary conclusion. If, as claimed by some, Samuel was in heaven, he must have been summoned thence, either by the power of God or by that of Satan. None can believe for a moment that Satan had power to call the holy prophet of God from heaven to honor the incantations of an abandoned woman. Nor can we conclude that God summoned him to the witch's cave; for the Lord had already refused to communicate with Saul by dreams, by Urim, or by prophets. These were God's own appointed mediums of communication, and he did not pass them by to deliver the message through the agent of Satan.

The message itself is sufficient evidence of its origin. Its object was not to lead Saul to repentance, but to urge him on to ruin; and this is not the work of God, but of Satan. Furthermore, the act of Saul in consulting a sorceress is cited in Scripture as one reason why he was rejected by God and abandoned to destruction. "Saul died for his transgression which he committed against the Lord, even against the word of the Lord, which he kept not, and also for asking counsel of one that had a familiar spirit, *to inquire of it*; and inquired not of the Lord; therefore he slew him, and turned the kingdom unto David the son of Jesse."1 Chron. 10:13, 14.—PP 683.

11.

Angels From David's Time to the Babylonian Captivity

David's Reign

The ark remained in the house of Abinadab until David was made king. He gathered together all the chosen men of Israel, thirty thousand, and went to bring up the ark of God. They sat the ark upon a new cart, and brought it out of the house of Abinadab. Uzzah and Ahio, sons of Abinadab, drave the cart. David and all the house of Israel played before the Lord on all manner of musical instruments. "And when they came to Nachon's threshing-floor, Uzzah put forth his hand to the ark of God, and took hold of it, for the oxen shook it. And the anger of the Lord was kindled against Uzzah, and God smote him there for his error; and there he died by the ark of God." Uzzah was angry with the oxen, because they stumbled. He showed a manifest distrust of God, as though He who had brought the ark from the land of the Philistines, could not take care of it. Angels who attended the ark struck down Uzzah for presuming impatiently to put his hand upon the ark of God.—4aSG 111.

With a view to extending his conquests among foreign nations, David determined to increase his army by requiring military service from all who were of proper age. To effect this, it became necessary to take a census of the population. It was pride and ambition that prompted this action of the king. . . .

The object of the undertaking was directly contrary to the principles of a theocracy. Even Joab remonstrated, unscrupulous as he had heretofore shown himself. . . . "Nevertheless the king's word prevailed against Joab." . . .

The next morning a message was brought to David by the prophet Gad: "Thus saith the Lord, Choose thee either three years' famine; or three months to be destroyed before thy foes, while that the sword of thine enemies overtaketh thee; or else three days the sword of the Lord, even the pestilence, in the land, and the angel of the Lord destroying throughout all the coasts of Israel. Now therefore," said the prophet, "advise thyself what word I shall bring again to him that sent me."

The king's answer was, . . . "Let us fall now into the hand of the Lord; for his mercies are great: and let me not fall into the hand of man."—PP 747, 748.

Swift destruction followed. Seventy thousand were destroyed by pestilence. David and the elders of Israel were in the deepest humiliation, mourning before the Lord. As the angel of the Lord was on his way to destroy Jerusalem, God bade him stay his work of death. . . . The angel, clad in warlike garments, with a drawn sword in his hand, stretched out over Jerusalem, is revealed to David, and to those who are with him. David is terribly afraid, yet he cries out in his distress and his compassion for Israel. He begs of God to save the sheep. In anguish he confesses, "I have sinned, and I have done wickedly; but these sheep, what have they done? Let thine hand, I pray thee, be against me, and against my father's house."—1SP 385, 386.

The destroying angel had stayed his course outside Jerusalem. He stood upon Mount Moriah, "in the threshing-floor of Ornan the Jebusite." Directed by the prophet, David went to the mountain, and there built an altar to the Lord, "and offered burnt offerings and peace offerings, and called upon the Lord; and he answered him from heaven by fire upon the altar of burnt offering." "So the Lord was entreated for the land, and the plague was stayed from Israel."

The spot upon which the altar was erected, henceforth ever to be regarded as holy ground, was tendered to the king by Ornan as a gift. But the king declined thus to receive it. . . . "David gave to Ornan for the place six hundred shekels of gold by weight." This spot, memorable as the place where Abraham had built the altar to offer up his son, and now hallowed by this great deliverance, was afterward chosen as the site of the temple erected by Solomon. . . .

From the very opening of David's reign, one of his most cherished plans had been that of erecting a temple to the Lord. Though he had not been permitted to execute this design, he had manifested no less zeal and earnestness in its behalf.—PP 748, 750.

The Lord, through His angel, instructed David, and gave him a pattern of the house which Solomon should build for Him. An angel was commissioned to stand by David while he was writing out, for the benefit of Solomon, the important directions in regard to the arrangements of the house.—4aSG 94.

Solomon

The hearts of the people were turned toward Solomon, as they were to David, and they obey him in all things. The Lord sends His angel to instruct Solomon by a dream, in the night season. He dreams that God converses with him. "And God said, Ask what I shall give thee. And Solomon said, Thou hast shewed unto thy servant David, my father, great mercy, according as he walked before thee in truth, and in righteousness, and in uprightness of heart with thee; and thou hast kept for him this great kindness, that thou hast given him a son to sit on his throne, as it is this day. . . . Give, therefore, thy servant an understanding heart to judge thy people, that I may discern between good and bad; for who is able to judge this thy so great a people?"—4aSG 96, 97.

In addition to the cherubim on the top of the ark, Solomon made two other angels of larger size, standing at each end of the ark, representing the heavenly angels always guarding the law of God. It is impossible to describe the beauty and splendor of this tabernacle. There, as in the tabernacle [in the wilderness], the sacred ark was borne in solemn, reverential order, and set in its place beneath the wings of the two stately cherubim that stood upon the floor.—1SP 413.

Elijah

After his first appearance to Ahab, denouncing upon him the judgments of God because of his and Israel's apostasy, God directed his course from Jezebel's power to a place of safety in the mountains, by the brook Cherith. There He honored Elijah by sending food to him morning and evening by an angel of heaven. Then, as the brook became dry, He sent him to the widow of Sarepta, and wrought a miracle daily to keep the widow's family and Elijah in food.—3T 288.

Facing King Ahab and the false prophets and surrounded by the assembled hosts of Israel, Elijah stands, the only one who has appeared to vindicate the honor of Jehovah. He whom the whole kingdom has charged with its weight of woe, is now before them, apparently defenseless in the presence of the monarch of Israel, the prophets of Baal, the men of war, and the surrounding thousands. But Elijah is not alone. Above and around him are the protecting hosts of heaven—angels that excel in strength.—PK 147.

In the full light of the sun, surrounded by thousands—men of war, prophets of Baal, and the monarch of Israel—stands the defenseless man, Elijah, apparently alone, yet not alone. The most powerful host of heaven surrounds him. Angels who excel in strength have come from heaven to shield the faithful and righteous prophet. With stern and commanding voice Elijah cries: "How long halt ye between two opinions? if the Lord be God, follow him: but if Baal, then follow him. And the people answered him not a word."—3T 280.

While Israel on Carmel doubt and hesitate, the voice of Elijah again breaks the silence: "I, even I only, remain a prophet of the Lord; but Baal's prophets are four hundred and fifty men. Let them therefore give us two bullocks; and let them choose one bullock for themselves, and cut it in pieces, and lay it on wood, and put no fire under: and I will dress the other bullock, and lay it on wood, and put no fire under: and call ye on the name of your gods, and I will call on the name of the Lord: and the God that answereth by fire, let him be God."—PK 148, 149.

How gladly would Satan, who fell like lightning from heaven, come to the help of those whom he had deceived, and whose minds he had controlled, and who were fully devoted to his service. Gladly would he have sent the lightning and kindled their sacrifices; but Jehovah had set Satan's bounds. He had restrained his power, and all his devices could not convey one spark to Baal's altars.—RH Sept. 30, 1873.

Did God forsake Elijah in his hour of trial? Oh, no! He loved His servant no less when Elijah felt himself forsaken of God and man, than when, in answer to his prayer, fire flashed from heaven and illuminated the mountain top. And now, as Elijah slept, a soft touch and a pleasant voice awoke him. He started up in terror, as if to flee, fearing that the enemy had discovered him. But the pitying face bending over him was not the face of an enemy, but of a friend. God had sent an angel from heaven with food for His servant. "Arise and eat," the angel said. "And he looked, and, behold, there was a cake baken on the coals, and a cruse of water at his head."

After Elijah had partaken of the refreshment prepared for him, he slept again. A second time the angel came. Touching the exhausted man, he said with pitying tenderness, "Arise and eat; because the journey is too great for thee." "And he arose, and did eat and drink"; and in the strength of that food he was able to journey "forty days and forty nights unto Horeb the mount of God," where he found refuge in a cave.—PK 166.

In the desert, in loneliness and discouragement [after his mountaintop experience on Mt. Carmel], Elijah had said that he had had enough of life and had prayed that he might die. But the Lord in His mercy had not taken him at his word. There was yet a great work for Elijah to do.—PK 228.

Through a mighty angel the word of the Lord came to him, "What doest thou here, Elijah?" In bitterness of soul, Elijah mourned out his complaint: "I have been very jealous for the Lord God of hosts: for the children of Israel have forsaken thy covenant, thrown down thine altars, and slain thy prophets with the sword: and I, even I only, am left; and they seek my life, to take it away."

Calling upon the prophet to leave the cave in which

he had hidden, the angel bade him stand before the Lord on the mount, and listen to His word. As Elijah obeyed, "behold, the Lord passed by, and a great and strong wind rent the mountains, and brake in pieces the rocks before the Lord; but the Lord was not in the wind: and after the wind an earthquake; but the Lord was not in the earthquake; and after the earthquake a fire; but the Lord was not in the fire: and after the fire a still small voice. And it was so, when Elijah heard it, that he wrapped his face in his mantle, and went out, and stood in the entering in of the cave." His petulance was silenced, his spirit softened and subdued. He now knew that a quiet trust, a firm reliance on God, would ever find for him a present help in time of need.—RH Oct. 23, 1913.

When Elijah was about to leave Elisha, he said to him, "Ask what I shall do for thee, before I be taken away from thee. And Elisha said, I pray thee, let a double portion of thy spirit be upon me." [2 Kings 2:9.] —GW (1915) 116.

"And he [Elijah] said, Thou hast asked a hard thing: nevertheless, if thou see me when I am taken from thee, it shall be so unto thee; . . . and it came to pass, as they still went on, and talked, that, behold, there appeared a chariot of fire, and horses of fire, and parted them both asunder; and Elijah went up by a whirlwind into heaven.

"And Elisha saw it, and he cried, My father, my father, the chariot of Israel, and the horsemen thereof!" —Ed 60.

Elisha

In Second Kings we read how holy angels came on a mission to guard the Lord's chosen servants. The prophet Elisha was in Dothan, and thither the king of . . . [Syria] sent horses and chariots and a great host to take him. "And when the servant of the man of God was risen early, and gone forth, behold an host compassed the city with horses and chariots. And his servant said unto him, Alas, my master! how shall we do?"—AUG Aug. 20, 1902.

"Fear not," was the answer of the prophet; "for they that be with us are more than they that be with them." And then, that the servant might know this for himself, "Elisha prayed, and said, Lord, I pray Thee, open his eyes, that he may see." "The Lord opened the eyes of the young man; and he saw: and, behold, the mountain was full of horses and chariots of fire round about Elisha." Between the servant of God and the hosts of armed foemen was an encircling band of heavenly angels. They had come down in mighty power, not to destroy, not to exact homage, but to encamp round about and minister to the Lord's weak and helpless ones. —PK 256, 257.

It was not given Elisha to follow his master in a fiery chariot. Upon him the Lord permitted to come a lingering illness. During the long hours of human weakness and suffering, his faith laid fast hold on the promises of God, and he beheld ever about him heavenly messengers of comfort and peace. As on the heights of

Dothan he had seen the encircling hosts of heaven, the fiery chariots of Israel and the horsemen thereof, so now he was conscious of the presence of sympathizing angels; and he was sustained.—PK 263, 264.

Isaiah

In Isaiah's day idolatry itself no longer provoked surprise. Iniquitous practices had become so prevalent among all classes, that the few who remained true to God were often tempted to lose heart, and to give way to discouragement and despair. . . .

Such thoughts as these were crowding through Isaiah's mind as he stood under the portico of the temple. Suddenly the gate and the inner veil of the temple seemed to be uplifted or withdrawn, and he was permitted to gaze within, upon the holy of holies, where even the prophet's feet might not enter. There rose up before him a vision of Jehovah sitting upon a throne high and lifted up, while the train of His glory filled the temple. On each side of the throne hovered the seraphim, their faces veiled in adoration, as they ministered before their Maker, and united in the solemn invocation, "Holy, holy, holy, is the Lord of hosts: the whole earth is full of His glory."—PK 306, 307.

An indescribable glory emanated from a personage on the throne, and His train filled the temple. . . . Cherubim were on either side of the mercy-seat, as guards round the great King, and they glowed with the glory that enshrouded them from the presence of God. As their songs of praise resounded in deep, earnest notes of adoration, the pillars of the gate trembled, as if shaken by an earthquake. These holy beings sang forth the praise and glory of God with lips unpolluted with sin. The contrast between the feeble praise which he [Isaiah] had been accustomed to bestow upon the Creator and the fervid praises of the seraphim, astonished and humiliated the prophet. He had for the time being, the sublime privilege of appreciating the spotless purity of Jehovah's exalted character.

While he listened to the song of the angels, as they cried, "Holy, holy, holy, is the Lord of hosts; the whole earth is full of his glory," the glory, the infinite power, and the unsurpassed majesty of the Lord passed before his vision, and was impressed upon his soul. In the light of this matchless radiance, that made manifest all he could bear in the revelation of the divine character, his own inward defilement stood out before him with startling clearness. His very words seemed vile to him.—RH Oct. 16, 1888.

The seraphim dwelt in the presence of Jesus, yet they veiled with their wings their faces and their feet. They looked upon the King in His beauty, and covered themselves. When Isaiah saw the glory of God, his soul was prostrated in the dust. Because of the unclouded vision he was graciously permitted to behold, he was filled with self-abasement. This will ever be the effect upon the human mind when the beams of the Sun of Righteousness shine gloriously upon the soul. . . . As the increasing glory of Christ is revealed, the human agent will see no glory in himself; for the concealed deformity of his soul is laid bare, and self-esteem and self-glorying are extinguished. Self dies, and Christ lives.—BE&ST Dec. 3, 1894.

Such was the prospect that greeted Isaiah when he was called to the prophetic mission; yet he was not discouraged, for ringing in his ears was the triumphal chorus of the angels surrounding the throne of God, "The whole earth is full of His glory." Isaiah 6:3. And his faith was strengthened by visions of the glorious conquests by the church of God, when "the earth shall be full of the knowledge of the Lord, as the waters cover the sea." Isaiah 11:9.—PK 371.

Ezekiel

Upon the banks of the river Chebar, Ezekiel beheld a whirlwind seeming to come from the north, "a great cloud, and a fire infolding itself, and a brightness was about it, and out of the midst thereof as the color of amber." A number of wheels intersecting one another were moved by four living beings. High above all these "was the likeness of a throne, as the appearance of a sapphire stone; and upon the likeness of the throne was the likeness as the appearance of a man above upon it." "And there appeared in the cherubims the form of a man's hand under their wings." Ezekiel 1:4, 26; 10:8.

The wheels were so complicated in arrangement that at first sight they appeared to be in confusion; yet they moved in perfect harmony. Heavenly beings, sustained and guided by the hand beneath the wings of the cherubim, were impelling those wheels; above them, upon the sapphire throne, was the Eternal One;

and round about the throne was a rainbow, the emblem of divine mercy.

As the wheel-like complications were under the guidance of the hand beneath the wings of the cherubim, so the complicated play of human events is under divine control. Amidst the strife and tumult of nations, He that sitteth above the cherubim still guides the affairs of this earth.—PK 535, 536.

12.

Angels From the Captivity to John the Baptist

Daniel and His Three Companions

The love and fear of God was before Daniel, and he educated and trained all his powers to respond as far as possible to the loving care of the Great Teacher, conscious of his amenability to God. The four Hebrew children would not allow selfish motives and love of amusements to occupy the golden moments of this life. They worked with a willing heart and ready mind. This is no higher standard than every Christian may attain. God requires of every Christian scholar more than has been given him. Ye are "a spectacle unto the world, and to angels, and to men."—FCE 192.

Those who do as Daniel and his fellows did will have the cooperation of God and the angels.—4MR 125.

Nebuchadnezzar's Fiery Furnace

As in the days of Shadrach, Meshach, and Abednego, so in the closing period of earth's history the Lord will work mightily in behalf of those who stand steadfastly for the right. He who walked with the Hebrew worthies in the fiery furnace will be with His followers wherever they are. His abiding presence will comfort and sustain. In the midst of the time of trouble—trouble such as has not been since there was a nation—His chosen ones will stand unmoved. Satan with all the hosts of evil cannot destroy the weakest of God's saints. Angels that excel in strength will protect them, and in their behalf Jehovah will reveal Himself as a "God of gods," able to save to the uttermost those who have put their trust in Him.—PK 513.

Belshazzar's Feast

While they were that night in the midst of idolatrous mirth, the king's countenance suddenly pales, and he seems paralyzed with terror; for lo! a bloodless hand is tracing mystic characters on the wall over against him. The revelers discern the curious and, to them, unintelligible writing. The exciting merriment dies away, and a painful silence falls upon the throng. The king's thoughts troubled him, "the joints of his loins were loosed, and his knees smote one against another." Trembling with alarm, he "cried aloud to bring in the astrologers, the Chaldeans, and the soothsayers. And the king spake, and said to the wise men of Babylon, Whosoever shall read this writing, and shew me the interpretation thereof, shall be clothed in scarlet, and have a chain of gold about his neck, and shall be the third ruler in the kingdom." But these men are no more able to interpret the mystic characters traced by the hand of an angel of God than they were to interpret the dream of Nebuchadnezzar.—*RH* Feb. 8, 1881.

There was a witness . . . in Belshazzar's palace at that festival. . . . The angel on that occasion traced the characters over against the walls of the palace.—*Ellen G. White 1888 Materials* 517.

Daniel in the Lions' Den

Daniel prayed unto his God three times a day. Satan is enraged at the sound of fervent prayer, for he knows that he will suffer loss. Daniel was preferred above the presidents and princes, because an excellent spirit was in him. Fallen angels feared his influence would weaken their control over the rulers of the kingdom. . . . The accusing host of evil angels stirred up the presidents and princes to envy and jealousy, and they watched Daniel closely to find some occasion against him that they might report him to the king, but they failed. Then these agents of Satan sought to make his faithfulness to God the cause of his destruction. Evil angels laid out the plan for them, and these agents readily carried it into effect. The king was ignorant of the subtle mischief purposed against Daniel.

With the full knowledge of the king's decree he [Daniel] still bows before his God, "his windows being open." He considers supplication to God of sufficient importance to sacrifice his life rather than to relinquish it. On account of his praying to God he was cast into the lions' den. Evil angels accomplished their purpose thus far. But Daniel continues to pray, even in the den of lions. . . . Did God forget him there? Oh no; Jesus the mighty Commander of the host of heaven, sent His angel to close the mouths of those hungry lions that they should not hurt the praying man of God, and all was peace in that terrible den. The king witnessed his preservation, and brought him out with honors. Satan and his angels were defeated and enraged. The agents Satan had employed were doomed to perish in the terrible manner they had plotted to destroy Daniel.—4bSG 85, 86.

Gabriel Sent to Explain the Vision of Daniel 8

Shortly before the fall of Babylon, when Daniel was meditating on these prophecies [of Isaiah and Jeremiah] and seeking God for an understanding of the times, a series of visions was given him concerning the rise and fall of kingdoms. With the first vision, as recorded in the seventh chapter of the book of Daniel, an interpretation was given; yet not all was made clear to the prophet. "My cogitations much troubled me," he wrote of his experience at the time, "and my countenance changed in me: but I kept the matter in my heart." Daniel 7:28.

Through another vision further light was thrown upon the events of the future; and it was at the close of this vision that Daniel heard "one saint speaking, and another saint said unto that certain saint which spake, How long shall be the vision?" The answer that was given, "Unto two thousand and three hundred days; then shall the sanctuary be cleansed," filled him with perplexity. Earnestly he sought for the meaning of the vision. He could not understand the relation sustained by the seventy years' captivity, as foretold through Jeremiah, to the twenty-three hundred years that in vision he heard the heavenly visitant declare should elapse before the cleansing of God's sanctuary. The angel Gabriel gave him a partial interpretation; yet when the prophet heard the words, "The vision . . . shall be for many days," he fainted away. . . .

Still burdened in behalf of Israel, Daniel studied anew the prophecies of Jeremiah. They were very plain. . . .

With faith founded on the sure word of prophecy, Daniel pleaded with the Lord for the speedy fulfillment of these promises.—PK 553, 554.

As Daniel's prayer is going forth, the angel Gabriel comes sweeping down from the heavenly courts, to tell him that his petitions are heard and answered. This mighty angel has been commissioned to give him skill and understanding—to open before him the mysteries of future ages. Thus, while earnestly seeking to know and understand the truth, Daniel was brought into communion with Heaven's delegated messenger.—RH Feb. 8, 1881.

Even before he [Daniel] had finished pleading with God, Gabriel again appeared to him and called his attention to the vision he had seen prior to the fall of Babylon at the death of Belshazzar. The angel then outlined in detail the period of the seventy weeks. —RH March 21, 1907.

The Struggle for Influence
Over the Kings of Persia

Heavenly agencies have to contend with hindrances before the purpose of God is fulfilled in its time. The king of Persia was controlled by the highest of all evil angels. He refused, as did Pharaoh, to obey the word of the Lord. Gabriel declared, He [Satan] withstood me twenty-one days by his representations against the Jews. But Michael came to his help, and then he remained with the kings of Persia, holding the powers in check, giving right counsel against evil counsel. —4BC 1173.

[Cyrus] the [Persian] monarch had resisted the impressions of the Spirit of God during the three weeks while Daniel was fasting and praying, but Heaven's Prince, the arch-angel, Michael, was sent to turn the heart of the stubborn king to take some decided action to answer the prayer of Daniel.—RH Feb. 8, 1881.

No less a personage than the Son of God appeared to Daniel. This description is similar to that given by John when Christ was revealed to him upon the Isle of Patmos.

Our Lord now comes with another heavenly messenger to teach Daniel what would take place in the latter days.—RH Feb. 8, 1881.

Daniel . . . could not look upon the angel's face, and he had no strength; it was all gone. So the angel came to him and set him upon his knees. He could not behold him then. And then the angel came to him with the appearance of a man. Then he could bear the sight.—2MR 348.

The victory was finally gained, and the forces of the enemy were held in check all the days of Cyrus, who reigned for seven years, and all the days of his son Cambyses, who reigned about seven years and a half. —RH Dec. 5, 1907.

The Second Temple

The second temple did not equal the first in magnificence, nor was it hallowed by those visible tokens of the divine presence which pertained to the first temple. There was no manifestation of supernatural power to mark its dedication. No cloud of glory was seen to fill the newly erected sanctuary. No fire from heaven descended to consume the sacrifice upon its altar. The Shekinah no longer abode between the cherubim in the most holy place; the ark, the mercy seat, and the tables of testimony were not found there. No sign from heaven made known to the inquiring priest the will of Jehovah.—PK 596, 597.

Ezra

The children of the captivity who had returned with Ezra "offered burnt offerings unto the God of Israel" for a sin offering and as a token of their gratitude and thanksgiving for the protection of holy angels during the journey.—PK 619.

Nehemiah

Four months Nehemiah waited for a favorable opportunity to present his request to the king. During this time, though his heart was heavy with grief, he endeavored to bear himself with cheerfulness in the royal presence. In those halls of luxury and splendor, all must appear lighthearted and happy. Distress must not cast its shadow over the countenance of any attendant of royalty. But in Nehemiah's seasons of retirement, concealed from human sight, many were the prayers, the confessions, the tears, heard and witnessed by God and angels.—PK 630.

The Visions of Zechariah

"I lifted up mine eyes again," says Zechariah, "and looked, and behold a man with a measuring line in his hand. Then said I, Whither goest thou? And he said unto me, To measure Jerusalem, to see what is the breadth thereof, and what is the length thereof. And, behold, the angel that talked with me went forth, and another angel went out to meet him, and said unto him, Run, speak to this young man, saying, Jerusalem shall be inhabited as towns without walls for the multitude of men and cattle therein: for I, saith the Lord, will be unto her a wall of fire round about, and will be the glory in the midst of her."—RH Dec. 26, 1907.

The Vision of Joshua and the Angel

The scene of Satan's accusation was presented before the prophet. He says, "He showed me Joshua the high priest standing before the angel of the Lord, and Satan standing at his right hand to resist him."—RH Aug. 22, 1893.

A most forcible and impressive illustration of the work of Satan and the work of Christ, and the power of our Mediator to vanquish the accuser of His people, is given in the prophecy of Zechariah. In holy vision the prophet beholds Joshua the high priest, "clothed with filthy garments," standing before the Angel of the Lord, entreating the mercy of God in behalf of His people who are in deep affliction. Satan stands at his right hand to resist him.

Because Israel has been chosen to preserve the knowledge of God in the earth, they had been, from their first existence as a nation, the special objects of Satan's enmity, and he had determined to cause their destruction. He could do them no harm while they were obedient to God; therefore he had bent all his power and cunning to entice them into sin. Ensnared by his temptations they had transgressed the law of God and thus separated from the Source of their strength, and had been left to become the prey of their heathen enemies. They were carried into captivity to Babylon, and there remained for many years.

Yet they were not forsaken of the Lord. His prophets were sent to them with reproofs and warnings. The people were awakened to see their guilt, they humbled themselves before God, and returned to Him with true repentance. Then the Lord sent them messages of encouragement, declaring that He would deliver them from their captivity and restore them to His favor. It was this that Satan was determined to prevent. A remnant of Israel had already returned to their own land, and Satan was seeking to move upon the heathen nations, who were his agents, to utterly destroy them. . . .

The high priest [Joshua] cannot defend himself or his people from Satan's accusations. He does not claim that Israel are free from fault. In his filthy garments, symbolizing the sins of the people, which he bears as their representative, he stands before the Angel, confessing their guilt, yet pointing to their repentance and humiliation, relying upon the mercy of a sin-pardoning Redeemer and in faith claiming the promises of God.

Then the Angel, who is Christ Himself, the Saviour of sinners, puts to silence the accuser of His people, declaring: "The Lord rebuke thee, O Satan; even the Lord that hath chosen Jerusalem rebuke thee: is not this a brand plucked out of the fire?" Israel had long remained in the furnace of affliction. Because of their sins they had been well-nigh consumed in the flame kindled by Satan and his agents for their destruction, but God had now set His hand to bring them forth. In their penitence and humiliation the compassionate Saviour will not leave His people to the cruel power of the heathen. . . .

As the intercession of Joshua is accepted, the command is given, "Take away the filthy garments from him," and to Joshua the Angel declares, "Behold, I have caused thine iniquity to pass from thee, and I will clothe thee with change of raiment." "So they set a fair miter upon his head, and clothed him with garments." His own sins and those of his people were pardoned. Israel

were clothed with "change of raiment"—the righteousness of Christ imputed to them. The miter placed upon
Joshua's head was such as was worn by the priests and
bore the inscription, "Holiness to the Lord," signifying
that, notwithstanding his former transgressions, he was
now qualified to minister before God in His sanctuary.

After thus solemnly investing him with the dignity
of the priesthood the Angel declared: "Thus saith the
Lord of hosts; If thou wilt walk in My ways, and if thou
wilt keep My charge, then thou shalt also judge My
house, and shalt also keep My courts, and I will give
thee places to walk among these that stand by." He
would be honored as the judge or ruler over the temple
and all its services; he should walk among attending
angels, even in this life, and should at last join the glorified throng around the throne of God.—5T 467-469.

This word of assurance is given to all who have faith
in God. Receive this wonderful promise. It is not a human being who is speaking. "Thus saith the Lord of
hosts: If thou wilt walk in my ways, and if thou wilt
keep my charge, then thou shalt also judge my house,
and shalt also keep my courts and I will give thee places
to walk among these that stand by."

"Among these that stand by." The hosts of the enemy, who are trying to bring God's people into disrepute, and the hosts of heaven, ten thousand times ten
thousand angels, who watch over and guard the
tempted people of God, uplifting them and strengthening them—these are they who stand by. And God says
to His believing ones, You shall walk among them. You
shall not be overcome by the powers of darkness. You

shall stand before me in the sight of the holy angels, who are sent forth to minister to those who shall be heirs of salvation.—RH April 30, 1901.

The Vision of the Seven Lamps and the Two Olive Trees

Immediately after Zechariah's vision of Joshua and the angel, given to the high priest as a personal testimony for his own encouragement and the encouragement of all the people of God, the prophet received a personal testimony regarding the work of Zerubbabel. "The angel that talked with me," Zechariah declares, "came again, and waked me, as a man that is waked out of his sleep, and said unto me, What seest thou? And I said, I have looked, and behold a candlestick all of gold, with a bowl upon the top of it, and his seven lamps thereon, and seven pipes to the seven lamps, which are upon the top thereof: and two olive trees by it, one upon the right side of the bowl, and the other upon the left side thereof."—RH Jan. 16, 1908.

"Then answered I, and said unto him, What are these two olive-trees upon the right side of the candlestick and upon the left side thereof? And I answered again, and said unto him, what be these two olive-branches which through the two golden pipes empty the golden oil out of themselves? and he answered me and said, ". . . . These are the two anointed ones, that stand by the Lord of the whole earth."

The anointed ones standing by the Lord of the whole earth have the position once given to Satan as covering cherub. By the holy beings surrounding His throne, the Lord keeps up a constant communication with the inhabitants of the earth.—RH July 20, 1897.

Angels in the Time of Esther

The king's [Ahasuerus'] decision against the Jews was secured under false pretenses through misrepresentation of that peculiar people. Satan instigated the scheme in order to rid the earth of those who preserved the knowledge of the true God. But his plots were defeated by a counterpower that reigns among the children of men. Angels that excel in strength were commissioned to protect the people of God, and the plots of their adversaries returned upon their own heads.—5T 450.

On the day appointed for their destruction, "the Jews gathered themselves together in their cities throughout all the provinces of the king Ahasuerus, to lay hand on such as sought their hurt: and no man could withstand them; for the fear of them fell upon all people." Angels that excel in strength had been commissioned by God to protect His people while they "stood for their lives." Esther 9:2, 16.—PK 602.

The Father of John the Baptist

Zacharias dwelt in "the hill country of Judea," but he had gone up to Jerusalem to minister for one week in the temple, a service required twice a year from the priests of each course. . . .

He was standing before the golden altar in the holy

place of the sanctuary. . . . Suddenly he became conscious of a divine presence. An angel of the Lord was "standing on the right side of the altar." The position of the angel was an indication of favor, but Zacharias took no note of this. For many years he had prayed for the coming of the Redeemer; now heaven had sent its messenger to announce that these prayers were about to be answered; but the mercy of God seemed too great for him to credit. He was filled with fear and self-condemnation.

But he was greeted with the joyful assurance: "Fear not, Zacharias; for thy prayer is heard; and thy wife Elizabeth shall bear thee a son, and thou shalt call his name John. . . . And Zacharias said unto the angel, Whereby shall I know this? for I am an old man, and my wife well stricken in years."

To the question of Zacharias, the angel said, "I am Gabriel, that stand in the presence of God; and am sent to speak unto thee, and to show thee these glad tidings." Five hundred years before, Gabriel had made known to Daniel the prophetic period which was to extend to the coming of Christ. The knowledge that the end of this period was near had moved Zacharias to pray for the Messiah's advent. Now the very messenger through whom the prophecy was given had come to announce its fulfillment.

The words of the angel, "I am Gabriel, that stand in the presence of God," show that he holds a position of high honor in the heavenly courts. When he came with a message to Daniel, he said, "There is none that holdeth with me in these things, but Michael your Prince." Dan. 10:21. Of Gabriel the Saviour speaks in the Revelation, saying that "He sent and signified it by His angel unto His servant John." Rev. 1:1. And to John the angel declared, "I am a fellow servant with thee and with thy brethren the prophets." Rev. 22:9, R.V. Wonderful thought—that the angel who stands next in honor to the Son of God is the one chosen to open the purposes of God to sinful men.—DA 97-99.

The work of John the Baptist was foretold by the angel who visited Zacharias in the temple. "Fear not, Zacharias," he said; "for thy prayer is heard; and thy wife Elizabeth shall bear thee a son, and thou shalt call his name John. And . . . he shall be filled with the Holy Ghost, . . . and many of the children of Israel shall he turn to the Lord their God. And he shall go before him in the spirit and power of Elias."—RH Feb. 20, 1900.

The angel Gabriel gave special directions to the parents of John in regard to temperance. A lesson was given upon health reform by one of the exalted angels from the throne of heaven.—2SP 43.

In John the Baptist, God raised up a messenger to prepare the way of the Lord. He was to bear to the world an unflinching testimony, reproving and denouncing sin. In announcing John's mission and work, the angel said: "He shall go before him [Christ] in the spirit and power of Elias, to turn the hearts of the fathers to the children, and the disobedient to the wisdom of the just; to make ready a people prepared for the Lord." —RH Aug. 2, 1898.

13.

The Incarnation and Early Life of Christ

The Incarnation a Profound Mystery

In contemplating the incarnation of Christ in humanity, we stand baffled before an unfathomable mystery that the human mind cannot comprehend. The more we reflect upon it, the more amazing does it appear. How wide is the contrast between the divinity of Christ and the helpless infant in Bethlehem's manger! How can we span the distance between the mighty God and a helpless child? And yet the Creator of worlds, He in whom was the fulness of the Godhead bodily, was manifest in the helpless babe in the manger. Far higher than any of the angels, equal with the Father in dignity and glory, and yet wearing the garb of humanity! Divinity and humanity were mysteriously combined, and man and God became one. It is in this union that we find the hope of our fallen race.—ST July 30, 1896.

The Universe Was Watching

The coming of Christ to our world was a great event, not only to this world, but to all the worlds in the universe of God. Before the heavenly intelligences He was to take upon Himself our nature, to be tempted in all points like as we are.—ST Feb. 20, 1893.

By coming to dwell with us, Jesus was to reveal God both to men and to angels. . . . But not alone for His earthborn children was this revelation given. Our little world is the lesson book of the universe. God's wonderful purpose of grace, the mystery of redeeming love, is the theme into which "angels desire to look," and it will be their study throughout endless ages.—DA 19, 20.

Why Christ Took Human Nature

He [Satan] had proudly boasted to the heavenly angels that when Christ should appear, taking man's nature, He would be weaker than himself, and he would overcome Him by his power. He exulted that Adam and Eve in Eden could not resist his insinuations when he appealed to their appetite.—RH July 28, 1874.

The only begotten Son of God came to our world as a man, to reveal to the world that men could keep the law of God. Satan, the fallen angel, had declared that no man could keep the law of God after the disobedience of Adam.—6MR 334.

Satan claimed that it was impossible for human beings to keep God's law. In order to prove the falsity of this claim, Christ left His high command, took upon Himself the nature of man, and came to the earth to stand at the head of the fallen race, in order to show that humanity could withstand the temptations of Satan.—UL 172.

Christ's Human Nature

His [Christ's] human nature was created; it did not even possess the angelic powers. It was human, identical with our own.—3SM 129.

Christ in the weakness of humanity was to meet the temptations of one possessing the powers of the higher nature that God had bestowed on the angelic family.—RH Jan. 28, 1909.

The story of Bethlehem is an exhaustless theme. In it is hidden "the depth of the riches both of the wisdom and knowledge of God." Romans 11:33. We marvel at the Saviour's sacrifice in exchanging the throne of heaven for the manger, and the companionship of adoring angels for the beasts of the stall. Human pride and self-sufficiency stand rebuked in His presence. Yet this was but the beginning of His wonderful condescension. It would have been an almost infinite humiliation for the Son of God to take man's nature, even when Adam stood in his innocence in Eden. But Jesus accepted humanity when the race had been weakened by four thousand years of sin. Like every child of Adam He accepted the results of the working of the great law of heredity. What these results were is shown in the history of His earthly ancestors. He came with such a heredity to share our sorrows and temptations, and to give us the example of a sinless life.—DA 48, 49.

As God, Christ could not be tempted any more than He was not tempted from His allegiance in heaven. But as Christ humbled Himself to the nature of man, He could be tempted. He had not taken on Him even the nature of the angels, but humanity, perfectly identical with our own nature, except without the taint of sin. A human body, a human mind, with all the peculiar properties, He was bone, brain, and muscle. A man of our flesh, He was compassed with the weakness of humanity. The circumstances of His life were of that character that He was exposed to all the inconveniences that belong to men, not in wealth, not in ease, but in poverty and want and humiliation. He breathed the very air man must breathe. He trod our earth as man. He had reason, conscience, memory, will, and affections of the human soul which was united with His divine nature.—16MR 181, 182.

In the Child of Bethlehem was veiled the glory before which angels bow. This unconscious babe was the promised seed, to whom the first altar at the gate of Eden pointed.—DA 52.

The Annunciation

Before His [Christ's] birth the angel had said to Mary, "He shall be great, and shall be called the Son of the Highest: and the Lord God shall give unto Him the throne of His father David: and He shall reign over the house of Jacob forever." Luke 1:32, 33. These words Mary had pondered in her heart; yet while she believed that her child was to be Israel's Messiah, she did not comprehend His mission.—DA 81, 82.

Angels behold the weary travelers, Joseph and Mary, making their way to the city of David, to be taxed, according to the decree of Caesar Augustus. Here, in the providence of God, Joseph and Mary had been brought; for this was the place prophecy had predicted that Christ should be born. They seek a place of rest at the inn, but are turned away because there is no room. The wealthy and honorable have been welcomed, and find refreshment and room, while these weary travelers are compelled to seek refuge in a coarse building which shelters the dumb beasts.—RH Dec. 17, 1872.

Before Christ's Birth

In heaven it was understood that the time had come for the advent of Christ to the world, and angels leave glory to witness His reception by those He came to bless and save. They had witnessed His glory in heaven, and they anticipate that He will be received with honor in accordance with His character and the dignity of His mission. As angels approach the earth, they first come to the people God had separated from the nations of the world as His peculiar treasure. They see no especial interest among the Jews, no eager waiting and watching that they may be the first to receive the Redeemer, and acknowledge His advent.—RH Dec. 17, 1872.

An angel visits the earth to see who are prepared to welcome Jesus. But he can discern no tokens of expectancy. He hears no voice of praise and triumph that the period of Messiah's coming is at hand. The angel hovers for a time over the chosen city and the temple where the divine presence has been manifested for ages; but even here is the same indifference. . . .

In amazement the celestial messenger is about to return to heaven with the shameful tidings, when he discovers a group of shepherds who are watching their flocks by night, and, as they gaze into the starry heavens, are contemplating the prophecy of a Messiah to come to earth, and longing for the advent of the world's Redeemer. Here is a company that is prepared to receive the heavenly messenger. And suddenly the angel of the Lord appears, declaring the good tidings of great joy.—GC 314.

The angels passed by the school of the prophets, the palaces of kings, and appeared to the humble shepherds, guarding their flocks by night, upon Bethlehem's plains. One angel first appeared, clothed with the panoply of heaven; and so surprised and so terrified were the shepherds that they could only gaze upon the wondrous glory of the heavenly visitant with unutterable amazement. The angel of the Lord came to them, and said, "Fear not, for, behold, I bring you tidings of great joy, which shall be unto all people; for unto you is born this day, in the city of David, a Saviour, who is Christ the Lord. And this shall be a sign unto you, Ye shall find the babe wrapped in swaddling clothes, lying in a manger."

No sooner had their eyes become accustomed to the glorious presence of the one angel, than, lo! the whole plain was lighted up with the wondrous glory of the multitude of angels that peopled the plains of Bethlehem. The angel quieted the fears of the shepherds before opening their eyes to behold the multitude of the heavenly host, all praising God, and saying, "Glory to God in the highest; and on earth, peace, good will to men."—RH Dec. 9, 1884.

The shepherds are filled with joy, and, as the bright glory disappears, and the angels return to heaven, they are all aglow with the glad tidings, and hasten in search of the Saviour. They find the infant Redeemer, as the celestial messengers had testified, wrapped in swaddling clothes, and lying in the narrow confines of a manger.—RH Dec. 17, 1872.

Satan saw the plains of Bethlehem illuminated with the brilliant glory of a multitude of heavenly angels. He heard their song, "Glory to God in the highest, and on earth peace, good will to men." The prince of darkness saw the amazed shepherds filled with fear as they beheld the illuminated plains. They trembled before the exhibitions of bewildering glory which seemed to entrance their senses. The rebel chief himself trembled at the proclamation of the angel to the shepherds, "Fear not; for, behold, I bring to you tidings of great joy, which shall be to all people. For unto you is born this day in the city of David a Saviour, which is Christ the Lord.". . .

The song of the heavenly messengers proclaiming the advent of the Saviour to a fallen world, and the joy expressed at this great event Satan knew boded no good to himself. Dark forebodings were awakened in his mind as to the influence this advent to the world would have upon his kingdom.—RH March 3, 1874.

The Magi

It was not alone upon the hills of Judea, not among the lowly shepherds only, that angels found the watchers for the Messiah's coming. In the land of the heathen also were those that looked for Him; they were wise men, rich and noble, the philosophers of the East. Students of nature, the Magi had seen God in His handiwork. From the Hebrew Scriptures they had learned of the Star to arise out of Jacob, and with eager desire they awaited His coming, who should be not only the "Consolation of Israel," but "a Light to lighten the Gentiles," and "for salvation unto the ends of the earth." Luke 2:25, 32; Acts 13:47.—GC 315.

The wise men . . . had studied prophecy, and knew the time was at hand when Christ would come, and they were anxiously watching for some sign of this great event, that they might be among the first to welcome the infant heavenly King, and worship Him. These wise men had seen the heavens illuminated with light,which enshrouded the heavenly messengers who heralded the advent of Christ to the shepherds of Israel, and after the angelic messenger returned to heaven, a luminous star appeared, and lingered in the heavens. The unusual appearance of the large, bright star which they had never seen before, hanging as a sign in the heavens, attracted their attention, and the Spirit of God moved them out to seek this heavenly Visitor to a fallen world.—*Redemption or the First Advent of Christ With His Life and Ministry* 16.

As the light [of the angels at Bethlehem] faded, a luminous star appeared, and lingered in the sky. It was not a fixed star nor a planet, and the phenomenon excited the keenest interest. That star was a distant company of shining angels, but of this the wise men were ignorant. Yet they were impressed that the star was of special import to them. They consulted priests and philosophers, and searched the scrolls of the ancient records. The prophecy of Balaam had declared, "There shall come a Star out of Jacob, and a Scepter shall rise out of Israel." Num. 24:17. Could this strange star have been sent as a harbinger of the Promised One? The magi had welcomed the light of heaven-sent truth; now it was shed upon them in brighter rays. Through dreams they were instructed to go in search of the newborn Prince.—DA 60.

Angels of God, in the appearance of a star, conducted the wise men on their mission in search of Jesus. They came with gifts and costly offerings of frankincense and myrrh, to pay their oblation to the infant King foretold in prophecy. They followed the brilliant messengers with assurance and great joy.—RH Dec. 9, 1884.

The wise men directed their course where the star seemed to lead them. As they drew nigh to the city of Jerusalem, the star was enshrouded in darkness, and no longer guided them. They reasoned that the Jews at Jerusalem could not be ignorant of the great event of the advent of the Messiah, and they made inquiries in the vicinity of Jerusalem. They plainly stated their errand. They were in search of Jesus, the king of the

Jews, for they had seen His star in the east, and had come to worship Him.—*Redemption or the First Advent of Christ With His Life and Ministry* 16.

The arrival of the magi was quickly noised throughout Jerusalem. Their strange errand created an excitement among the people, which penetrated to the palace of King Herod. The wily Edomite was aroused at the intimation of a possible rival. . . .

Herod suspected the priests of plotting with the strangers to excite a popular tumult and unseat him from the throne. He concealed his mistrust, however, determined to thwart their schemes by superior cunning. Summoning the chief priests and the scribes, he questioned them as to the teaching of their sacred books in regard to the place of the Messiah's birth.

This inquiry from the usurper of the throne, and made at the request of strangers, stung the pride of the Jewish teachers. The indifference with which they turned to the rolls of prophecy enraged the jealous tyrant. He thought them trying to conceal their knowledge of the matter. With an authority they dared not disregard, he commanded them to make close search, and to declare the birthplace of their expected King. "And they said unto him, In Bethlehem of Judea: for thus it is written by the prophet." . . .

The priests and elders of Jerusalem were not as ignorant concerning the birth of Christ as they pretended. The report of the angels' visit to the shepherds had been brought to Jerusalem, but the rabbis had treated it as unworthy of their notice. They themselves might have found Jesus, and might have been ready to lead the magi to His birthplace; but instead of this, the wise men came to call their attention to the birth of the Messiah. "Where is He that is born King of the Jews?" they said; "for we have seen His star in the East, and are come to worship Him."

Now pride and envy closed the door against the light. If the reports brought by the shepherds and the wise men were credited, they would place the priests and rabbis in a most unenviable position, disproving their claim to be the exponents of the truth of God. These learned teachers would not stoop to be instructed by those whom they termed heathen. It could not be, they said, that God had passed them by to communicate with ignorant shepherds or uncircumcised Gentiles. They determined to show their contempt for the reports that were exciting King Herod and all Jerusalem. They would not even go to Bethlehem to see whether these things were so. . . .

The wise men departed alone from Jerusalem. The shadows of night were falling as they left the gates, but to their great joy they again saw the star, and were directed to Bethlehem. They had received no such intimation of the lowly estate of Jesus as was given to the shepherds. . . . At Bethlehem they found no royal guard stationed to protect the newborn King. None of the world's honored men were in attendance. Jesus was cradled in a manger. His parents, uneducated peasants, were His only guardians. . . .

"When they were come into the house, they saw the young child with Mary His mother, and fell down, and worshiped Him." Beneath the lowly guise of Jesus, they recognized the presence of Divinity.—DA 61-63.

After the mission of the wise men had been accomplished, they were purposing to return, and bear the joyful news to Herod of the success of their journey. But God sent His angels in the night season to turn the course of the wise men. In the vision of the night they were plainly told not to return to Herod. They obeyed the heavenly messengers, and returned to their homes another way.—*Redemption or the First Advent of Christ With His Life and Ministry* 19.

In like manner Joseph received warning to flee into Egypt with Mary and the child. And the angel said, "Be thou there until I bring thee word: for Herod will seek the young child to destroy Him." Joseph obeyed without delay, setting out on the journey by night for greater security. . . .

Herod in Jerusalem impatiently awaited the return of the wise men. As time passed, and they did not appear, his suspicions were roused. . . . Soldiers were at once sent to Bethlehem, with orders to put to death all the children of two years and under.—DA 64-66.

But a higher power was at work against the plans of the prince of darkness. Angels of God frustrated his designs, and protected the life of the infant Redeemer. —ST Aug. 4, 1887.

Joseph, who was still in Egypt, was now bidden by an angel of God to return to the land of Israel; . . . but learning that Archelaus reigned in Judea in his father's stead, he feared that the father's designs against Christ might be carried out by the son. . . .

Again Joseph was directed to a place of safety. He returned to Nazareth, his former home, and here for nearly thirty years Jesus dwelt. . . . God . . . commissioned angels to attend Jesus and protect Him till He should accomplish His mission on earth, and die by the hands of those whom He came to save.—DA 66, 67.

The Silent Years

From His earliest years, He [Christ] lived a life of toil. The greater part of His earthly life was spent in patient work in the carpenter's shop at Nazareth. In the garb of a common laborer the Lord of life trod the streets of the little town in which He lived, going to and returning from His humble toil; and ministering angels attended Him as He walked side by side with peasants and laborers, unrecognized and unhonored. —RH Oct. 3, 1912.

Throughout His [Christ's] childhood and youth, He manifested the perfection of character that marked His after life. He grew in wisdom and knowledge. As He witnessed the sacrificial offerings, the Holy Spirit taught Him that His life was to be sacrificed for the life of the world. He grew up as a tender plant, not in the large and noisy city, that is full of confusion and strife, but in the retired valleys among the hills. He was guarded from His earliest years by heavenly angels, yet His life was one long struggle against the powers of darkness. Satanic agencies combined with human instrumentalities to make His life one of temptation and trial. Through supernatural agencies, His words, which were life and salvation to all who receive and practice them, were perverted and misinterpreted.—ST Aug. 6, 1896.

Jesus made the lowly paths of human life sacred by His example. For thirty years He was an inhabitant of Nazareth. His life was one of diligent industry. He, the Majesty of heaven, walked the streets, clad in the simple garb of a common laborer. He toiled up and down the mountain steeps, going to and from His humble work. Angels were not sent to bear Him on their pinions up the tiresome ascents, or to lend their strength in performing His lowly task. Yet when He went forth to contribute to the support of the family by His daily toil, He possessed the same power as when He wrought the miracle of feeding the five thousand hungry souls on the shore of Galilee.—HR Oct. 1, 1876.

14.

Angels at Christ's Baptism and in the Wilderness

Christ's Baptism

When Jesus came to be baptized, John recognized in Him a purity of character that he had never before perceived in any man. . . . As Jesus asked for baptism, John drew back exclaiming, "I have need to be baptized of Thee, and comest Thou to me?" With firm yet gentle authority, Jesus answered, "Suffer it to be so now: for thus it becometh us to fulfill all righteousness." And John, yielding, led the Saviour down into the Jordan, and buried Him beneath the water. "And straightway coming up out of the water," Jesus "saw the heavens opened, and the Spirit like a dove descending upon Him."—DA 110, 111.

Heavenly angels were looking with intense interest upon the scene of the Saviour's baptism, and could the eyes of those who were looking on, have been opened, they would have seen the heavenly host surrounding the Son of God as He bowed on the banks of the Jordan.—YI June 23, 1892.

The Saviour's glance seems to penetrate heaven as He pours out His soul in prayer. Well He knows how sin has hardened the hearts of men, and how difficult it will be for them to discern His mission, and accept the gift of salvation. He pleads with the Father for power to overcome their unbelief, to break the fetters with which Satan has enthralled them, and in their behalf to conquer the destroyer. He asks for the witness that God accepts humanity in the person of His Son.

Never before have the angels listened to such a prayer. They are eager to bear to their loved Commander a message of assurance and comfort. But no; the Father Himself will answer the petition of His Son. Direct from the throne issue the beams of His glory. The heavens are opened, and upon the Saviour's head descends a dovelike form of purest light—fit emblem of Him, the meek and lowly One. . . .

The people stood silently gazing upon Christ. His form was bathed in the light that ever surrounds the throne of God. His upturned face was glorified as they had never before seen the face of man. From the open heavens a voice was heard saying, "This is My beloved Son, in whom I am well pleased."—DA 111, 112.

The Lord had promised to give John a sign whereby he might know who was the Messiah, and now as Jesus went up out of the water, the promised sign was given; for he saw the heavens opened, and the Spirit of God, like a dove of burnished gold, hovered over the head of Christ, and a voice came from heaven, saying, "This is My beloved Son, in whom I am well pleased."—YI June 23, 1892.

Of the vast throng at the Jordan, few except John discerned the heavenly vision.—DA 112.

At the Saviour's baptism, Satan was among the witnesses. He saw the Father's glory overshadowing His Son. He heard the voice of Jehovah testifying to the divinity of Jesus. Ever since Adam's sin, the human race had been cut off from direct communion with God; the interaction between heaven and earth had been through Christ; but now that Jesus had come "in the likeness of sinful flesh" (Rom. 8:3), the Father Himself spoke. He had before communicated with humanity *through* Christ; now He communicated with humanity *in* Christ. Satan had hoped that God's abhorrence of evil would bring an eternal separation between heaven and earth. But now it was manifest that the connection between God and man had been restored.—DA 116.

Satan could see through His [Christ's] humanity the glory and purity of the One with whom he had been associated in the heavenly courts. There rose before the tempter a picture of what he himself then was, a covering cherub, possessing beauty and holiness. —BE&ST July 23, 1900.

Christ's Threefold Temptation in the Wilderness

Satan had declared to his associate angels that he would overcome Christ on the point of appetite. He hoped to gain a victory over Him in His weakness. —ST April 4, 1900.

Satan saw that he must either conquer or be conquered. The issues of the conflict involved too much to be entrusted to his confederate angels. He must personally conduct the warfare.—DA 116.

While in the wilderness, Christ fasted, but He was insensible to hunger. . . . He spent the time in earnest prayer, shut in with God. It was as if He were in the presence of His Father. . . . The thought of the warfare before Him made Him oblivious to all else, and His soul was fed with the bread of life. . . . He saw the breaking of Satan's power over fallen and tempted ones. He saw Himself healing the sick, comforting the hopeless, cheering the desponding, and preaching the gospel to the poor—doing the work that God had outlined for Him; and He did not realize any sense of hunger until the forty days of His fast were ended.

The vision passed away, and then, with strong craving, Christ's human nature called for food. Now was Satan's opportunity to make his assault. He resolved to appear as one of the angels of light that had appeared to Christ in His vision.—21MR 8, 9.

Suddenly an angel appears before Him [Christ], apparently one of the angels that He saw not long since. . . . The words from heaven, "This is My beloved Son, in whom I am well pleased," were still sounding in the ears of Satan. But he was determined to make Christ disbelieve this testimony.—21MR 9.

Satan appeared to Him [Christ] . . . as a beautiful angel from heaven, claiming that he had a commission from God to declare the Saviour's fast at an end.—RH Jan. 14, 1909.

He [Satan] told the Redeemer that He need fast no longer, that His long abstinence was accepted by the Father, that He had gone far enough, and that He was at liberty to work a miracle in His own behalf.—ST July 29, 1889.

Believing that the angelic character he [Satan] had assumed defied detection, he now feigned to doubt the divinity of Christ.—2SP 91.

The First Temptation

Satan reasoned with Christ thus: If the words spoken after His baptism were indeed the words of God, that He was the Son of God, He need not bear the sensations of hunger; He could give him proofs of His divinity by showing His power in changing the stones of that barren wilderness into bread.—*Redemption or the First Advent of Christ With His Life and Ministry* 48.

Satan told Christ that He was only to set His feet in the blood-stained path, but not to travel it. Like Abraham He was tested to show His perfect obedience. He also stated that he was the angel that stayed the hand of Abraham as the knife was raised to slay Isaac, and he had now come to save His [Christ's] life; that it was not necessary for Him to endure the painful hunger and death from starvation; he would help Him bear a part of the work in the plan of salvation.—RH Aug. 4, 1874.

He [Satan] then called the attention of Christ to his own attractive appearance, clothed with light and strong in power. He claimed to be a messenger direct from the throne of Heaven, and asserted that he had a right to demand of Christ evidences of His being the Son of God.—RH Aug. 4, 1874.

It was by . . . [Satan's] words, not by his appearance, that the Saviour recognized the enemy.—RH July 22, 1909.

In taking the nature of man, Christ was not equal in appearance with the angels of heaven, but this was one of the necessary humiliations that He willingly accepted when He became man's Redeemer. Satan urged that if He was indeed the Son of God He should give him some evidence of His exalted character. He suggested that God would not leave His Son in so deplorable a condition. He declared that one of the heavenly angels had been exiled to earth, and His appearance indicated that instead of being the King of Heaven He was that fallen angel. He called attention to his own beautiful appearance, clothed with light and strength, and insultingly contrasted the wretchedness of Christ with his own glory.—2SP 91.

The Second Temptation

"Then the devil taketh Him up into the holy city, and setteth Him on a pinnacle of the temple, and saith unto Him, If Thou be the Son of God, cast Thyself down: for it is written, "He shall give His angels charge concerning Thee: and in their hands they shall bear Thee up, lest at any time Thou dash Thy foot against a stone."—DA 124.

Satan, to manifest his strength, carried Jesus to Jerusalem, and set Him upon a pinnacle of the temple. —1SG 32.

He [Satan] again demanded of Christ, if He was indeed the Son of God, to give him evidence by casting Himself from the dizzy height upon which he had placed Him. He urged Christ to show His confidence in the preserving care of His Father by casting Himself down from the temple. In Satan's first temptation upon the point of appetite, he had tried to insinuate doubts in regard to God's love and care for Christ as His Son, by presenting His surroundings and His hunger as evidence that He was not in favor with God. He was unsuccessful in this. He next tried to take advantage of the faith and perfect trust Christ had shown in His heavenly Father to urge Him to presumption. "If thou be the Son of God, cast thyself down; for it is written, He shall give his angels charge concerning thee; and in their hands they shall bear thee up, lest at any time thou dash thy foot against a stone."—RH Aug. 18, 1874.

The wily foe himself presents words that proceeded from the mouth of God. He still appears as an angel of light, and he makes it evident that he is acquainted with the Scriptures, and understands the import of what is written. As Jesus before used the Word of God to sustain His faith, the tempter now uses it to countenance his deception. He claims that he has been only testing the fidelity of Jesus, and he now commends His steadfastness. As the Saviour has manifested trust in God, Satan urges Him to give still another evidence of His faith.

But again the temptation is prefaced with the insinuation of distrust. "*If* Thou be the Son of God." Christ was tempted to answer the "if," but He refrained from the slightest acceptance of the doubt. He would not imperil His life in order to give evidence to Satan.—DA 124.

When Satan quoted the promise, "He shall give His angels charge concerning Thee," he omitted the words, "to keep Thee in all Thy ways"; that is, in all the ways of God's choosing. Jesus refused to go outside the path of obedience. While manifesting perfect trust in His Father, He would not place Himself unbidden in a position that would necessitate the interposition of His Father to save Him from death. He would not force Providence to come to His rescue, and thus fail of giving man an example of trust and submission.—ST Dec. 10, 1902.

If Jesus had cast Himself from the pinnacle, it would not have glorified His Father; for none would witness the act but Satan, and the angels of God. And it would be tempting the Lord to display His power to His bitterest foe. It would have been condescending to the one whom Jesus came to conquer.—1SG 33.

The Third Temptation

Jesus was victor in the second temptation, and now

Satan manifests himself in his true character. But he does not appear as a hideous monster, with cloven feet and bat's wings. He is a mighty angel, though fallen. He avows himself the leader of rebellion and the god of this world.

Placing Jesus upon a high mountain, Satan caused the kingdoms of the world, in all their glory, to pass in panoramic view before Him.—DA 129.

In his first two temptations, he [Satan] had concealed his true character and purpose, claiming to be an exalted messenger from the courts of heaven. But he now throws off all disguise, avowing himself the Prince of Darkness, and claiming the earth for his dominion.—2SP 95.

The great deceiver sought to blind the eyes of Christ by the glitter and tinsel of the world, and presented before Him the kingdoms of this world and the glory of them. He who had fallen from heaven, pictured the world as possessing the gilding of the world above, in order that he might induce Christ to accept the bribe, and fall down and worship him.—ST March 28, 1895.

The sunlight lay on templed cities, marble palaces, fertile fields, and fruit-laden vineyards. The traces of evil were hidden. The eyes of Jesus, so lately greeted by gloom and desolation, now gazed upon a scene of unsurpassed loveliness and prosperity. Then the tempter's voice was heard: "All this power will I give Thee, and the glory of them: for that is delivered unto me; and to whomsoever I will I give it. If Thou therefore wilt worship me, all shall be Thine." . . .

Now the tempter offered to yield up the power he had usurped. Christ might deliver Himself from the dreadful future by acknowledging the supremacy of Satan. But to do this was to yield the victory in the great controversy.—DA 129.

Calling him [Satan] by his true name, Jesus rebukes the deceiver. Divinity flashed through suffering humanity, and He made manifest through His word the authority of heaven. He reveals to the deceiver that, though he had resumed the disguise of an angel of light, his true character was not hidden from the Saviour of the world. He called him Satan, the angel of darkness, who had left his first estate, and had refused allegiance to God.—ST March 28, 1895.

Satan left the field a vanquished foe, peremptorily dismissed. At the word of Christ, "Get thee hence, Satan," the powerful fallen angel had no choice but to obey. Angels that excel in strength were on the battleground, guarding the interest of the tempted soul, and ready to resist the foe.—RH April 24, 1894.

Heavenly Angels Watched Christ Being Tempted

Apparently Christ was alone with him [Satan] in the wilderness of temptation. Yet He was not alone, for angels were round Him just as angels of God are commissioned to minister unto those who are under the fearful assaults of the enemy.—16MR 180.

All heaven watched the conflict between the Prince of light and the prince of darkness. Angels stood ready to interpose in Christ's behalf should Satan pass the prescribed limit.—BE&ST Sept. 3, 1900.

These were real temptations, no pretense. Christ "suffered being tempted" (Heb. 2:18). Angels of heaven were on the scene on that occasion, and kept the standard uplifted, that Satan should not exceed his bounds and overpower the human nature of Christ.—1SM 94.

The strain upon Christ had left Him as one dead. "And, behold, angels came and ministered unto Him." Their arms encircled Him. Upon the breast of the highest angel in heaven His head rested. . . . The foe was vanquished.—BE&ST Sept. 3, 1900.

After Satan had ended his temptations, he departed from Jesus for a season, and angels prepared Him food in the wilderness.—EW 158.

After the Third Temptation

After Satan had failed to overcome Christ in the wilderness, he combined his forces to oppose Him in His ministry, and if possible to thwart His work. What he could not accomplish by direct, personal effort, he determined to effect by strategy. No sooner had he withdrawn from the conflict in the wilderness than in council with his confederate angels he matured his plans for still further blinding the minds of the Jewish people, that they might not recognize their Redeemer. He planned to work through his human agencies in the religious world, by imbuing them with his own enmity against the champion of truth. He would lead them to reject Christ and to make His life as bitter as possible, hoping to discourage Him in His mission.—DA 205, 206.

15.

Good and Evil Angels During Christ's Ministry

Devil Possession in Jesus' Day

The period of Christ's personal ministry among men was the time of greatest activity for the forces of the kingdom of darkness. For ages Satan with his evil angels had been seeking to control the bodies and the souls of men, to bring upon them sin and suffering.—DA 257.

The deception of sin had reached its height [by the time Christ began His ministry]. All the agencies for depraving the souls of men had been put in operation. . . . Satanic agencies were incorporated with men. The bodies of human beings, made for the dwelling place of God, had become the habitation of demons. The senses, the nerves, the passions, the organs of men, were worked by supernatural agencies in the indulgence of the vilest lust. The very stamp of demons was impressed upon the countenances of men. Human faces reflected the expression of the legions of evil with which they were possessed. . . .

Satan was exulting that he had succeeded in debasing the image of God in humanity. Then Jesus came to restore in man the image of his Maker. . . . He came to expel the demons that had controlled the will. He came to lift us up from the dust, to reshape the marred character after the pattern of His divine character, and make it beautiful with His own glory.—DA 36-38.

The fact that men have been possessed with demons is clearly stated in the New Testament. The persons thus afflicted were not merely suffering with disease from natural causes. Christ had perfect understanding of that with which He was dealing, and He recognized the direct presence and agency of evil spirits. —4SP 332.

Satan and his angels were very busy during Christ's ministry, inspiring men with unbelief, hate, and scorn.—1SG 36.

Rejection at Nazareth

During His childhood and youth, Jesus had worshiped among His brethren in the synagogue at Nazareth. Since the opening of His ministry He had been absent from them, but they had not been ignorant of what had befallen Him. As He again appeared among them, their interest and expectation were excited to the highest pitch. . . .

When a rabbi was present at the synagogue, he was expected to deliver the sermon, and any Israelite might give the reading from the prophets. Upon this Sabbath Jesus was requested to take part in the service. He "stood up to read. And there was delivered unto Him a roll of the prophet Isaiah." Luke 4:16, 17, R.V., margin. . . .

Jesus stood before the people as a living expositor of the prophecies concerning Himself. Explaining the words He had read, He spoke of the Messiah as a reliever of the oppressed, a liberator of captives, a healer of the afflicted, restoring sight to the blind, and revealing to the world the light of truth. . . . As their hearts were moved upon by the Holy Spirit, they responded with fervent amens and praises to the Lord.—DA 236, 237.

The Spirit witnessed so powerfully to His [Christ's] claims that the hearts of all who were in the synagogue responded to the gracious words that proceeded from His lips. Here was the turning point with that company. As Christ's divinity flashed through humanity, their spiritual sight was quickened. A new power of discernment and appreciation came upon them, and the conviction was almost irresistible that Jesus was the Son of God. But Satan was at hand to arouse doubts, unbelief, and pride.—ST Sept. 14, 1882.

When Jesus announced, "This day is this scripture fulfilled in your ears," they were suddenly recalled to think of themselves, and of the claims of Him who had been addressing them.—DA 237.

Who is this Jesus? they questioned. He who had claimed for Himself the glory of the Messiah was the son of a carpenter, and had worked at His trade with His father Joseph. . . . Although His life had been spotless, they would not believe that He was the Promised One. . . .

As they opened the door to doubt, their hearts became so much the harder for having been momentarily softened. Satan was determined that blind eyes should not that day be opened, nor souls bound in slavery be set at liberty. With intense energy he worked to fasten them in unbelief. . . .

The words of Jesus to His hearers in the synagogue struck at the root of their self-righteousness, pressing home upon them the bitter truth that they had departed from God and forfeited their claim to be His people. . . . They now scorned the faith with which Jesus had at first inspired them. They would not admit that He who had sprung from poverty and lowliness was other than a common man.—DA 237-239.

Angels of light were in that assembly, watching with intense interest the decision of the hour. Angels of Satan also were on the ground to suggest doubts and arouse prejudice. . . .

From unbelief sprung malice. That a man who had sprung from poverty and a lowly birth should dare to reprove them, filled the hearts of the Nazarenes with hatred amounting to madness. The assembly broke up in confusion. The people laid hands on Jesus, thrusting Him from the synagogue and out of their city.—ST June 16, 1887.

All seemed eager for His destruction. They hurried Him to the brow of a steep precipice, intending to cast Him headlong from it. Shouts and maledictions filled the air. Some were casting stones and dirt at Him; but suddenly He disappeared out of their midst, they knew not how, or when. Angels of God attended Jesus in the midst of that infuriated mob, and preserved His life. The heavenly messengers were by His side in the synagogue, while He was speaking; and they accompanied Him when pressed and urged on by the unbelieving, infuriated Jews. These angels blinded the eyes of that maddened throng, and conducted Jesus to a place of safety.—2SP 114, 115.

The Demoniac in the Synagogue at Capernaum

Jesus in the synagogue spoke of the kingdom He had come to establish, and of His mission to set free the captives of Satan. He was interrupted by a shriek of terror. A madman rushed forward from among the people, crying out, "Let us alone; what have we to do with Thee, Thou Jesus of Nazareth? art Thou come to destroy us? I know Thee who Thou art; the Holy One of God."

All was now confusion and alarm. The attention of the people was diverted from Christ, and His words were unheeded. This was Satan's purpose in leading his victim to the synagogue. But Jesus rebuked the demon, saying, "Hold thy peace, and come out of him. And when the devil had thrown him in the midst, he came out of him, and hurt him not."

The mind of this wretched sufferer had been darkened by Satan, but in the Saviour's presence a ray of light had pierced the gloom. He was roused to long for freedom from Satan's control; but the demon resisted the power of Christ. When the man tried to appeal to Jesus for help, the evil spirit put words into his mouth, and he cried out in an agony of fear. The demoniac partially comprehended that he was in the presence of One who could set him free; but when he tried to come within reach of that mighty hand, another's will held him, another's words found utterance through him. The conflict between the power of Satan and his own desire for freedom was terrible.—DA 255.

He who conquered the archenemy in the wilderness, wrested this writhing captive from the grasp of Satan. Jesus well knew that although assuming another form, this demon was the same evil spirit that had tempted Him in the wilderness.—2SP 180.

The demon exerted all his power to retain control of his victim. To lose ground here would be to give Jesus a victory. It seemed that the tortured man must lose his life in the struggle with the foe that had been the ruin of his manhood. But the Saviour spoke with authority, and set the captive free. The man who had been possessed stood before the wondering people happy in the freedom of self-possession. . . . The eye that had so lately glared with the fire of insanity, now beamed with intelligence, and overflowed with grateful tears.—DA 256.

The Healing of the Centurion's Servant

The centurion saw with the eye of faith that the angels of God were all around Jesus, and that His word would commission an angel to go to the sufferer. He knew that His word would enter the chamber, and that his servant would be healed.—RH March 11, 1890.

The Demoniacs of Gadara

In the early morning the Saviour and His companions came to shore. . . . From some hiding place among the tombs, two madmen rushed upon them as if to tear them in pieces. Hanging about these men were parts of chains which they had broken in escaping from confinement. Their flesh was torn and bleeding where they had cut themselves with sharp stones. Their eyes glared out from their long and matted hair; the very likeness of humanity seemed to have been blotted out by the demons that possessed them, and they looked more like wild beasts than like men.

The disciples and their companions fled in terror; but presently they noticed that Jesus was not with them, and they turned to look for Him. He was standing where they had left Him. He who had stilled the tempest, who had before met Satan and conquered him, did not flee before these demons. When the men, gnashing their teeth, and foaming at the mouth, approached Him, Jesus raised that hand which had beckoned the waves to rest, and the men could come no nearer. They stood raging but helpless before Him.

With authority He bade the unclean spirits come out of them. His words penetrated the darkened minds of the unfortunate men. They realized dimly that One was near who could save them from the tormenting demons. They fell at the Saviour's feet to worship Him; but when their lips were opened to entreat His mercy, the demons spoke through them, crying vehemently, "What have I to do with Thee, Jesus, Thou Son of God most high? I beseech Thee, torment me not." . . .

Upon a mountainside not far distant a great herd of swine was feeding. Into these the demons asked to be allowed to enter, and Jesus suffered them. Immediately a panic seized the herd. They rushed madly down the cliff, and, unable to check themselves upon the shore, plunged into the lake, and perished.

Meanwhile, a marvelous change had come over the demoniacs. Light had shone into their minds. Their eyes beamed with intelligence. The countenances, so long deformed into the image of Satan, became suddenly mild, the bloodstained hands were quiet, and with glad voices the men praised God for their deliverance. . . . Now these men were clothed and in their right mind, sitting at the feet of Jesus, listening to His words, and glorifying the name of Him who had made them whole.—DA 336-338.

The Healing of the Demoniac Son

The boy was brought, and as the Saviour's eyes fell upon him, the evil spirit cast him to the ground in convulsions of agony. He lay wallowing and foaming, rending the air with unearthly shrieks.

Again the Prince of life and the prince of the powers of darkness had met on the field of battle. . . . Angels of light and the hosts of evil angels, unseen, were pressing near to behold the conflict. For a moment, Jesus permitted the evil spirit to display his power, that the beholders might comprehend the deliverance about to be wrought. . . .

Jesus turns to the suffering one, and says, "Thou dumb and deaf spirit, I charge thee, come out of him,

and enter no more into him." There is a cry, an agonized struggle. The demon, in passing, seems about
to rend the life from his victim. Then the boy lies
motionless, and apparently lifeless. The multitude
whisper, "He is dead." But Jesus takes him by the
hand, and lifting him up, presents him, in perfect
soundness of mind and body, to his father. Father
and son praise the name of their Deliverer.—DA 428,
429.

Jesus Is Accused of Being Demon Possessed

Jesus declared Himself to be the True Shepherd, because He gave His life for the sheep. . . . Jesus spoke
these words in the hearing of a large concourse of people,
and a deep impression was made upon the hearts of
many who listened. The scribes and Pharisees were filled
with jealousy because He was regarded with favor by
many. . . . While He represented Himself as the True
Shepherd, the Pharisees said, "He hath a devil, and is
mad; why hear ye him?" But others distinguished the
voice of the True Shepherd, and said:
"These are not the words of him that hath a devil.
Can a devil open the eyes of the blind? And it was at
Jerusalem the feast of the dedication, and it was win-
ter. And Jesus walked in the temple in Solomon's porch.
Then came the Jews round about him, and said unto
him, How long dost thou make us to doubt? If thou be
the Christ, tell us plainly. Jesus answered them, I told
you, and ye believed not; the works that I do in my
Father's name, they bear witness of me. . . . I and my
Father are one." . . .

The Jews understood His meaning, . . . and they took up stones to stone Him. Jesus looked upon them calmly and unshrinkingly, and said, "Many good works have I showed you from my Father; for which of these works do ye stone me?"

The Majesty of heaven stood, calmly assured, as a god before His adversaries. Their scowling faces, their hands filled with stones, did not intimidate Him. He knew that unseen forces, legions of angels, were around about Him, and at one word from His lips they would strike with dismay the throng, should they offer to cast upon Him a single stone.—ST Nov. 27, 1893.

Although Jesus gave evidence of His divine power, yet He was not permitted to teach His lessons without interruption. The rulers sought to hold Him up to ridicule before the people. They would not allow Him to state His ideas and doctrines in a connected way, but, although frequently interrupted, light flashed into the minds of hundreds, and when the rulers heard the words of Jesus, that were clothed with power and held the people spellbound, they were angry, and said, "Thou art a Samaritan, and hast a devil." Jesus met these charges with quiet dignity, fearlessly and decidedly claiming that covenant rights were centered in Himself, and were not received through Abraham. He declared, "Before Abraham was, I am." The fury of the Jews knew no bounds, and they prepared to stone Him, but the angels of God, unseen by men, hurried Him out of their assembly.—ST May 26, 1890.

Evil Angels in Human Form
Were Among Christ's Hearers

Mingling with His [Christ's] hearers were angels in the form of men, making their suggestions, criticizing, misapplying, and misinterpreting the Saviour's words.—RH Aug. 11, 1903.

Christ was the instructor in the assemblies of these angels before they fell from their high estate.—3SM 410.

The Resurrection of Lazarus

Christ could have commanded the stone to remove, and it would have obeyed His voice. He could have bidden the angels who were close by His side to do this. At His bidding, invisible hands would have removed the stone. But it was to be taken away by human hands. Thus Christ would show that humanity is to cooperate with divinity. What human power can do divine power is not summoned to do.—DA 535.

Jesus Hunted From City
to City During His Ministry

Jesus was hunted from place to place during His ministry. Priests and rulers were on His track. They misrepresented His mission and labor. He came unto His own and His own received Him not. Angels watched the conflict at every step. They saw the spirit and work of the enemy. They looked with amazement upon the devices of Satan against the divine Son of God. They saw that he who had only been second to Jesus in power and glory had fallen so low that he could influence men to hunt the steps of Christ from city to city.—ST Nov. 25, 1889.

Again and again He [Jesus] would have been killed had it not been for the heavenly angels who attended Him and guarded His life until the time when the case of the Jews as a nation should be decided.—RH Oct. 12, 1897.

16.

Angels From Christ's Passion Until His Death

Jesus and His Disciples Go to Gethsemane

In company with His disciples, the Saviour slowly made His way to the garden of Gethsemane. The Passover moon, broad and full, shone from a cloudless sky. . . . As they approached the garden, the disciples had marked the change that came over their Master. Never before had they seen Him so utterly sad and silent. As He proceeded, this strange sadness deepened. . . .

Near the entrance to the garden, Jesus left all but three of the disciples, bidding them pray for themselves and for Him. With Peter, James, and John, He entered its secluded recesses. . . .

"Tarry ye here," He said, "and watch with Me."

He went a little distance from them . . . and fell prostrate upon the ground. He felt that by sin He was being separated from His Father. The gulf was so broad, so black, so deep, that His spirit shuddered before it. . . .

As Christ felt His unity with the Father broken up, He feared that in His human nature He would be unable to endure the coming conflict with the powers of darkness. In the wilderness of temptation the destiny of

the human race had been at stake. Christ was then conqueror. Now the tempter had come for the last fearful
struggle. For this he had been preparing during the three
years of Christ's ministry. Everything was at stake with
him. If he failed here, his hope of mastery was lost; the
kingdoms of the world would finally become Christ's; he
himself would be overthrown and cast out. But if Christ
could be overcome, the earth would become Satan's kingdom, and the human race would be forever in his power.
With the issues of the conflict before Him, Christ's soul
was filled with dread of separation from God. Satan told
Him that if He became the surety for a sinful world, the
separation would be eternal. . . .

In its hardest features Satan pressed the situation
upon the Redeemer: The people who claim to be above
all others in temporal and spiritual advantages have
rejected You. . . . One of Your own disciples . . . will
betray You. One of Your most zealous followers will deny
You. All will forsake You. . . .

In His agony He clings to the cold ground, as if to
prevent Himself from being drawn farther from
God. . . . From His pale lips comes the bitter cry, "O My
Father, if it be possible, let this cup pass from Me." Yet
even now He adds, "Nevertheless not as I will, but as
Thou wilt."—DA 685-687.

Angels in Gethsemane

The heavenly universe had watched with intense
interest the entire life of Christ—every step from the
manger to the present awful scene. And what a scene
was this for ten thousand times ten thousands of

angels, of cherubim and seraphim, to look upon.—ST
Dec. 9, 1897.

Angels were hovering over the place [Gethsemane],
witnessing the scene.—1SG 47.

They beheld the Son of God, their loved Commander,
in His superhuman agony apparently dying on the field
of battle to save a lost and perishing world. All heaven
had listened to that prayer of Christ.

His soul agony, which three times forced from His
pale and quivering lips the cry, "O my Father, if it be
possible, let this cup pass from me; nevertheless not as
I will, but as thou wilt," convulsed all heaven. They
saw their Lord inclosed by legions of Satanic forces,
His human nature weighed down with a shuddering,
mysterious dread.—ST Dec. 9, 1897.

The angels who had done Christ's will in heaven
were anxious to comfort Him; but it was beyond their
power to alleviate His sorrow. They had never felt the
sins of a ruined world, and they beheld with astonishment the object of their adoration subject to a grief beyond all expression. Though the disciples had failed to
sympathize with their Lord in the trying hour of His
conflict, all heaven was full of sympathy and waiting
the result with painful interest.—PT Dec. 3, 1885.

Thrice the prayer for deliverance had been wrung
from His [Christ's] lips. Heaven had been unable to
longer endure the sight, and had sent a messenger of
consolation to the prostrate Son of God, fainting and

dying under the accumulated guilt of the world.—PT Feb. 18, 1886.

In the supreme crisis, when heart and soul are breaking under the load of sin, Gabriel is sent to strengthen the divine Sufferer, and brace Him to tread His bloodstained path.—ST Dec. 9, 1897.

In this awful crisis, when everything was at stake, when the mysterious cup trembled in the hand of the Sufferer, the heavens opened, a light shone forth amid the stormy darkness of the crisis hour, and the mighty angel who stands in God's presence, occupying the position from which Satan fell, came to the side of Christ. The angel came not to take the cup from Christ's hand, but to strengthen Him to drink it, with the assurance of the Father's love. . . .

The sleeping disciples had been suddenly awakened by the light surrounding the Saviour. They saw the angel bending over their prostrate Master. They saw him lift the Saviour's head upon his bosom, and point toward heaven. They heard his voice, like sweetest music, speaking words of comfort and hope. . . . Again the disciples in their weariness yield to the strange stupor that overpowers them. Again Jesus finds them sleeping.

Looking sorrowfully upon them He says, "Sleep on now, and take your rest: behold, the hour is at hand, and the Son of man is betrayed into the hands of sinners."

Even as He spoke these words, He heard the footsteps of the mob in search of Him, and said, "Rise, let us be going: behold, he is at hand that doth betray me."

No traces of His recent agony were visible as Jesus stepped forth to meet His betrayer. Standing in advance of His disciples He said, "Whom seek ye?" They answered, "Jesus of Nazareth." Jesus replied, "I am He." —DA 693, 694.

It was in the power of Christ to deliver Himself. When He spoke the words, "I am He," immediately angels surrounded Him, and that throng had all the evidence they could or would have that Christ was the power of God.—TDG 267.

It was difficult for the angels to endure the sight. They would have delivered Jesus . . . but the commanding angels forbade them. . . . Jesus knew that angels were witnessing the scene of His humiliation. . . . The feeblest angel could have caused that multitude to fall powerless, and deliver Jesus.—1SG 50, 51.

The angel who had lately ministered to Jesus moved between Him and the mob. A divine light illuminated the Saviour's face, and a dovelike form overshadowed Him. In the presence of this divine glory, the murderous throng could not stand for a moment. They staggered back. Priests, elders, soldiers, and even Judas, fell as dead men to the ground. . . . But quickly the scene changed.—DA 694, 695.

The angel withdrew, and left Jesus standing calm and self-possessed, with the bright beams of the moon upon His pale face, and still surrounded by prostrate, helpless men, while the disciples were too much amazed to utter a word. As the angel removes, the hardened Roman soldiers start to their feet, and, with the priest and Judas, they gather about Christ as though ashamed of their weakness, and fearful that He would yet escape out of their hands.—ST Aug. 21, 1879.

The disciples had thought that their Master would not suffer Himself to be taken. . . . They were disappointed and indignant as they saw the cords brought forward to bind the hands of Him whom they loved. Peter in his anger rashly drew his sword and . . . cut off an ear of the high priest's servant. When Jesus saw what was done, He released His hands, . . . and saying, "Suffer ye thus far," He touched the wounded ear, and it was instantly made whole. He then said to Peter, "Put up again thy sword into his place: . . . Thinkest thou that I cannot now pray to My Father, and He shall presently give Me more than twelve legions of angels?"—DA 696.

As these words were spoken, the countenances of the angels were animated. They wished then, and there, to surround their Commander, and disperse that angry mob. But again sadness settled upon them as Jesus added, But how then shall the scriptures be fulfilled, that thus it must be? The hearts of the disciples sunk again in despair and bitter disappointment, as Jesus suffered them [the mob] to lead Him away.—1SG 48.

Before the Court of Annas and Caiaphas

Christ was to be tried formally before the Sanhedrin;

but before Annas He was subjected to a preliminary trial. . . .

When the council had assembled in the judgment hall, Caiaphas took his seat as presiding officer. . . . As Caiaphas . . . looked upon the prisoner, he was struck with admiration for His noble and dignified bearing. A conviction came over him that this Man was akin to God. The next instant he scornfully banished the thought. —DA 698, 703, 704.

All heaven saw the cruel work done to Christ. In the dreadful scenes transacted in the judgment hall, God showed to the heavenly universe the spirit that would be manifested by those that are unwilling to yield obedience to His law.—12MR 412.

It was difficult for the angels to endure the sight. They would have delivered Jesus out of [the] hands [of His inquisitors]; but the commanding angels forbade them. . . . Jesus knew that angels were witnessing the scene of His humiliation.

There stood Jesus, meek and humble before the infuriated multitude, while they offered Him the meanest abuse. They spit in His face—that face which they will one day desire to be hid from, which will give light to the city of God, and shine brighter than the sun—but not an angry look did He cast upon the offenders. He meekly raised His hand, and wiped it off. They covered His head with an old garment; blindfolded Him, and then struck Him in the face, and cried out, Prophesy unto us who it was that smote thee. There was commotion among the angels. They would have rescued

Him instantly; but their commanding angel restrained them.—1SG 50, 51.

Before Pilate

Men were imbued with a satanic spirit at the time when they decided that they would have Barabbas, a thief and murderer, in preference to the Son of God. The demoniac power triumphed over humanity; legions of evil angels took entire control of men, and in answer to Pilate's question as to whom he should release unto them, they shrieked out, "Away with this man, and release unto us Barabbas." When Pilate spoke again to them concerning Jesus, the hoarse cry was raised, "Crucify him, crucify him." Through yielding to demoniac agencies, men were led to take their stand on the side of the great apostate.

Unfallen worlds looked upon the scene with amazement, unable to comprehend the degradation that sin had wrought. Legions of evil angels controlled the priests and rulers, and gave voice to the suggestions of Satan in persuading and tempting the people by falsehoods and bribes to reject the Son of God, and to choose a robber and murderer in His stead. . . . What a scene was this for God to look upon, for seraphim and cherubim to behold! The only begotten Son of God, the Majesty of heaven, the King of glory, was mocked, insulted, taunted, rejected, and crucified by those whom He came to save, who had given themselves to the control of Satan.—RH April 14, 1896.

The angels who were witnessing the whole scene

noticed the convictions of Pilate, and marked his sympathy for Jesus. . . .

Satan and his angels were tempting Pilate, and trying to lead him on to his own ruin. They suggested to him that if he did not take any part in condemning Jesus, others would.—1SG 54, 56.

Even now Pilate was not left to act blindly. A message from God warned him from the deed he was about to commit. In answer to Christ's prayer, the wife of Pilate had been visited by an angel from heaven, and in a dream she had beheld the Saviour and conversed with Him. . . . She saw Him on trial in the judgment hall. She saw the hands tightly bound as the hands of a criminal. She saw Herod and his soldiers doing their dreadful work. She heard the priests and rulers, filled with envy and malice, madly accusing. She heard the words, "We have a law, and by our law He ought to die."

She saw Pilate give Jesus to the scourging, after he had declared, "I find no fault in Him." She heard the condemnation pronounced by Pilate, and saw him give Christ up to His murderers. She saw the cross uplifted on Calvary. She saw the earth wrapped in darkness, and heard the mysterious cry, "It is finished." Still another scene met her gaze. She saw Christ seated upon the great white cloud, while the earth reeled in space, and His murderers fled from the presence of His glory. With a cry of horror she awoke, and at once wrote to Pilate words of warning.

While Pilate was hesitating as to what he should do, a messenger pressed through the crowd, and handed him the letter from his wife, which read:

"Have thou nothing to do with that just Man: for I have suffered many things this day in a dream because of Him."

Pilate's face grew pale. He was confused by his own conflicting emotions. But while he had been delaying to act, the priests and rulers were still further inflaming the minds of the people. . . .

Pilate longed to deliver Jesus. But he saw that he could not do this, and yet retain his own position and honor. Rather than lose his worldly power, he chose to sacrifice an innocent life. . . .

Pilate yielded to the demands of the mob. Rather than risk losing his position, he delivered Jesus up to be crucified.—DA 732, 733, 738.

Christ's Crucifixion

The Son of God was delivered to the people to be crucified. . . . They laid on Him the heavy cross . . . but Jesus fainted beneath the burden. They then seized . . . a man who had not openly professed faith in Christ, yet believed on Him. They laid on him the cross and he bore it to the fatal spot. Companies of angels were marshaled in the air above the place.—1SG 57.

Who witnessed these scenes? The heavenly universe, God the Father, Satan and his angels.—BE&ST May 29, 1899.

Heavenly angels . . . heard the mocking taunts and saw the wagging of heads. Gladly would they have broken their ranks and gone to the Son of God in His humiliation and bodily anguish, but this they were not permitted to do.—18MR 71.

"He saved others; himself he cannot save," was the mocking taunt hurled at Christ during the agony of His death on the cross. At any moment He could have saved Himself, and come down from the cross; but had He done this, the world would have been given over to the control of the great apostate. It was a marvel to the angels that Christ did not seal with death the lips of the scoffers.—YI June 14, 1900.

By those who mocked Christ as He hung on the cross, Satan and his angels were personified. He filled them with vile and loathsome speeches. He inspired their taunts.—18MR 72.

The principalities and powers of darkness assembled round His cross. The arch apostate, still retaining his lofty stature, led the apostate host, who were leagued with human beings in the strife against God.—ST April 14, 1898.

He [Christ] was struggling with the power of Satan, who was declaring that he had Christ in his power, that he was superior in strength to the Son of God, that the Father had disowned His Son, and that He was no longer in the favor of God any more than himself.—2T 214.

Christ yielded not to the torturing foe, even in his bitterest anguish. Legions of evil angels were all about

Him; yet the holy angels were bidden not to break their ranks, and engage in conflict with the taunting, railing adversary, nor were they permitted to minister to the anguished spirit of the divine Sufferer. It was in this terrible hour of darkness, the face of His Father hidden, legions of evil angels enshrouding Him, the sins of the world upon Him, that from His pale lips were wrenched the words, "My God, my God, why hast thou forsaken me?"—BE&ST Jan. 1, 1887.

The darkness that covered the earth at His crucifixion concealed the company of heaven's powerful agencies, but the earth quaked at the tread of the heavenly throng. The rocks were rent; for three hours the earth was shrouded in impenetrable darkness; nature with her dark robes hid the sufferings of the Son of God. —5MR 353.

The Father, with His heavenly angels, was enclosed in that thick darkness. God was close beside His Son, though not manifesting Himself to Him or to any human being. Had one ray of His glory and power penetrated the thick cloud that enveloped Him, every spectator would have been extinguished.—12MR 385.

How could heaven keep silent? Can we wonder at the horrible unnatural darkness that hung over the cross? Can we wonder at the rending rocks, the rolling thunder, the flashing lightning, the shaking of the earth beneath the tread of the heavenly army as they beheld their loved Commander suffering such indignity?—RH Sept. 1, 1891.

When Christ cried out, "It is finished," the unfallen worlds were made secure. For them the battle was fought and the victory won. Henceforth Satan had no place in the affections of the universe.—RH March 12, 1901.

The holy angels were horror-stricken that one of their number could fall so far as to be capable of such cruelty as had been manifested toward the Son of God on Calvary. Every sentiment of pity and sympathy which they had ever felt for Satan in his exile was quenched in their hearts.—ST Sept. 23, 1889.

It was not the hand of the priest that rent from top to bottom the gorgeous veil that divided the holy from the most holy place. It was the hand of God. When Christ cried out, "It is finished," the Holy Watcher that was an unseen guest at Belshazzar's feast pronounced the Jewish nation to be a nation unchurched. The same hand that traced on the wall the characters that recorded Belshazzar's doom and the end of the Babylonian kingdom, rent the veil of the temple from top to bottom.—5BC 1109.

They [the Jewish leaders] took His body down, and laid it in Joseph's new tomb, and rolled a great stone to the door of the sepulcher, stating as their reasons for so doing that His disciples would come and steal Him away by night. Evil angels exulted around that sepulcher, because they thought that Christ had been overcome. A body of Roman soldiers had been stationed to guard the tomb, and the greatest precautions had been exercised by the Jews to make their triumph complete. But heavenly angels were guarding the place where their beloved Commander slept.—RH Oct. 9, 1888.

Not until the death of Christ was the character of Satan clearly revealed to the angels or to the unfallen worlds. Then the prevarications and accusations of him who had once been an exalted angel were seen in their true light.—ST Aug. 27, 1902.

The death of Christ upon the cross made sure the destruction of him who has the power of death, who was the originator of sin. When Satan is destroyed, there will be none to tempt to evil; the atonement will never need to be repeated; and there will be no danger of another rebellion in the universe of God. That which alone can effectually restrain from sin in this world of darkness, will prevent sin in heaven.

The significance of the death of Christ will be seen by saints and angels. Fallen men could not have a home in the paradise of God without the Lamb slain from the foundation of the world. . . . The angels ascribe honor and glory to Christ, for even they are not secure except by looking to the sufferings of the Son of God. It is through the efficacy of the cross that the angels of heaven are guarded from apostasy. Without the cross they would be no more secure against evil than were the angels before the fall of Satan. Angelic perfection failed in heaven. Human perfection failed in Eden. . . . The plan of salvation, making manifest the justice and love of God, provides an eternal safeguard against defection in unfallen worlds. . . . The death of Christ on the cross of Calvary is our only hope in this world, and it will be our theme in the world to come.—ST Dec. 30, 1889.

Christ, in His life and His death, has forever settled the deep and comprehensive question whether there is self-denial with God, and whether God is light and love. This was the question agitated in the heavens above, which was the beginning of Satan's alienation from God. The change or abolition of the laws of His government in the heavenly courts was demanded as the evidence of the love of God.—RH Oct. 21, 1902.

17.

Angels From Christ's Resurrection Until His Ascension

The Morning of Christ's Resurrection

The disciples rested on the Sabbath, sorrowing for the death of their Lord, while Jesus, the King of glory, lay in the tomb. As night drew on, soldiers were stationed to guard the Saviour's resting place, while angels, unseen, hovered above the sacred spot.—EW 181.

The night of the first day of the week had worn slowly away. The darkest hour, just before daybreak, had come. Christ was still a prisoner in His narrow tomb. The great stone was in its place; the Roman seal was unbroken; the Roman guards were keeping their watch. And there were unseen watchers. Hosts of evil angels were gathered about the place. Had it been possible, the prince of darkness with his apostate army would have kept forever sealed the tomb that held the Son of God. But a heavenly host surrounded the sepulcher. Angels that excel in strength were guarding the tomb, and waiting to welcome the Prince of life.—DA 779.

While it was yet dark, the watching angels knew that the time for the release of God's dear Son, their beloved Commander, had nearly come. As they were waiting with the deepest emotion the hour of His triumph, a mighty angel came flying swiftly from heaven.—EW 181.

The mightiest angel from heaven, he who held the position from which Satan fell, received his commission from the Father, and clothed with the panoply of heaven, he parted the darkness from his track. His face was like the lightning, and his garments white as snow.—5BC 1110.

One of the angelic host who had witnessed the scene of Jesus' humiliation, and was watching His sacred resting place, joined the angel from heaven, and together they came down to the sepulcher. The earth shook and trembled as they approached, and there was a mighty earthquake.—1SG 66.

The face they [the Roman soldiers] look upon is not the face of mortal warrior; it is the face of the mightiest of the Lord's host. This messenger is he who fills the position from which Satan fell. It was he who on the hills of Bethlehem proclaimed Christ's birth. The earth trembles at his approach, the hosts of darkness flee.—DA 779, 780.

The angel approached the grave, rolled away the stone as though it had been a pebble, and sat upon it. The light of heaven encircled the tomb, and the whole heaven was lighted by the glory of the angels.—5BC 1110.

The angelic commander laid hold of the great stone which had required many strong men to place it in position, rolled it away, and took his seat upon it, while his companion entered the sepulcher and unwound the wrappings from the face and head of Jesus.

Then the mighty angel, with a voice that caused the earth to quake, was heard: Jesus, thou Son of God, thy Father calls thee! Then He who had earned the power to conquer death and the grave came forth, with the tread of a conqueror, from the sepulcher, amid the reeling of the earth, the flashing of lightning, and the roaring of thunder.—3SP 192.

He who said, "I lay down my life, that I might take it again," came forth from the grave to life that was in Himself. Humanity died; divinity did not die. In His divinity, Christ possessed the power to break the bonds of death.—YI Aug. 4, 1898.

Christ in His Godhead shone forth as He burst from the tomb, and rose triumphant over death and the grave.—ST May 30, 1895.

The Roman guard . . . were enabled to endure the sight, for they had a message to bear as witnesses of the resurrection of Christ.—5BC 1110.

Terrible fear seized the guard. Where now was their power to keep the body of Jesus? They did not think of their duty, or of the disciples stealing Him away. They were amazed and affrighted, as the exceeding bright light of the angels shone all around brighter than the sun. The Roman guard saw the angels, and fell as dead men to the ground.—1SG 66.

In solemn awe the angelic host gazed upon the scene. And as Jesus walked forth from the sepulcher in majesty, those shining angels prostrated themselves to the ground and worshiped Him; then hailed Him with songs of victory and triumph.—1SG 66, 67.

The soldiers . . . heard the inhabitants of heaven singing with great joy and triumph: Thou hast vanquished Satan and the powers of darkness! Thou hast swallowed up death in victory! "And I heard a loud voice saying in heaven, Now is come salvation and strength, and the kingdom of our God, and the power of his Christ; for the accuser of our brethren is cast down, who accused them before our God day and night." —3SP 194.

As the angelic host passed back to heaven, and the light and glory passed away, [the Roman guard] raised themselves to see if it were safe for them to look around. They were filled with amazement as they saw that the great stone was rolled from the door of the sepulcher, and Jesus was risen.—1SG 68.

Satan did not now triumph. His angels had fled before the bright, penetrating light of the heavenly angels. They bitterly complained to their king, that their prey had been taken violently from them, and that He whom they so much hated had risen from the dead. —1SG 67.

Immediately After Christ's Resurrection

For a little while Satan seemed sad and showed distress. He held a council with his angels to consider what they should engage in next to work against the government of God. Said Satan, You must hasten to the chief priests and elders. We succeeded in deceiving them and blinding their eyes, and hardening their hearts against Jesus. We made them believe He was an impostor. That Roman guard will carry the hateful news that Christ is risen. We led the priests and elders on to hate Jesus, and to murder Him. Now hold it before them in a bright light, that as they were His murderers, if it becomes known that Jesus is risen, they will be stoned to death by the people, in that they killed an innocent man.—1SG 67, 68.

They [the Roman guards] turned from the sepulcher, overwhelmed by what they had seen and heard, and made their way with all haste to the city, relating to those whom they met the marvelous scenes they had witnessed. . . . Meanwhile a messenger was dispatched to the priests and rulers, announcing to them: Christ whom ye crucified is risen from the dead!

A servant was immediately sent with a private message summoning the Roman guard to the palace of the high priest. There they were closely questioned; they gave a full statement of what they had witnessed at the sepulcher: That an awful messenger had come from heaven with face like the lightning for brightness, and with garments white as snow; that the earth shook and trembled, and they were stricken powerless; that the angel had laid hold of the immense stone at the door of the sepulcher, and had rolled it away as if it had been a pebble; that a form of great glory had emerged from the sepulcher; that a chorus of voices had made the heavens and earth vocal with songs of victory and joy; that when the light had faded out, and the music had ceased, they had recovered their strength, found the tomb empty, and the body of Jesus nowhere to be found.—*Redemption: Or the Resurrection of Christ; and His Ascension*, section 6, pp. 14, 15.

They [the Roman guard] hastened to the chief priests and elders with the wonderful story of what they had seen; and as those murderers heard the marvelous report, paleness sat upon every face. Horror seized them at what they had done. They then realized that if the report was correct, they were lost. For a little while they were stupefied, and looked one to the other in silence, not knowing what to do or say. They were placed where they could not believe unless it be to their own condemnation.

They went aside by themselves to consult what should be done. They decided that if it should be spread abroad that Jesus had risen, and the report of such amazing glory, which caused the guard to fall like dead men, should come to the people, they would surely be enraged, and would slay them. They decided to hire the soldiers to keep the matter secret. They offered them much money, saying, Say ye, His disciples came by night and stole him away while we slept. And when the guard inquired what should be done with them for sleeping at their post, the priest and elders said that they would persuade the governor and save them.—1SG 68.

The Women Come to the Sepulcher

The women who had stood by the cross of Christ waited and watched for the hours of the Sabbath to pass. On the first day of the week, very early, they made their way to the tomb, taking with them precious spices to anoint the Saviour's body. . . .

Ignorant of what was even then taking place, they drew near the garden, saying as they went, "Who shall roll us away the stone from the door of the sepulcher?" They knew that they could not remove the stone, yet they kept on their way. And lo, the heavens were suddenly alight with glory that came not from the rising sun. The earth trembled. They saw that the great stone was rolled away. The grave was empty.

The women had not all come to the tomb from the same direction. Mary Magdalene was the first to reach the place; and upon seeing that the stone was removed, she hurried away to tell the disciples. Meanwhile the other women came up. A light was shining about the tomb, but the body of Jesus was not there. As they lingered about the place, suddenly they saw that they were not alone. A young man clothed in shining garments was sitting by the tomb. It was the angel who had rolled away the stone. He had taken the guise of humanity that he might not alarm these friends of Jesus. Yet about him the light of the heavenly glory was still shining.—DA 788, 789.

The women were greatly terrified, and bowed their faces to the earth; for the sight of the heavenly being was more than they could endure. The angel was compelled to hide his glory still more before he could converse with them.—YI July 21, 1898.

"Fear not ye," he said; "for I know that ye seek Jesus, which was crucified. He is not here: for He is risen, as He said. Come, see the place where the Lord lay. And go quickly, and tell His disciples that He is risen from the dead."

Again they look into the tomb, and again they hear the wonderful news. Another angel in human form is there, and he says, "Why seek ye the living among the dead? He is not here, but is risen: remember how He spake unto you when He was yet in Galilee, saying, The Son of man must be delivered into the hands of sinful men, and be crucified, and the third day rise again."

He is risen, He is risen! The women repeat the words again and again.—DA 789.

Christ's Ascension to His Father

"Go your way," the angels had said to the women, "tell His disciples and Peter that He goeth before you into Galilee: there shall ye see Him, as He said unto you." These angels had been with Christ as guardian angels throughout His life on earth. They had witnessed His trial and crucifixion. They had heard His words to His disciples.—DA 793.

Quickly the women departed from the sepulcher

"with fear and great joy; and did run to bring His disciples word."

Mary had not heard the good news. She went to Peter and John with the sorrowful message, "They have taken away the Lord out of the sepulcher, and we know not where they have laid Him."

The disciples hurried to the tomb, and found it as Mary had said. They saw the shroud and the napkin, but they did not find their Lord. . . .

Mary had followed John and Peter to the tomb; when they returned to Jerusalem, she remained. As she looked into the empty tomb, grief filled her heart. Looking in, she saw the two angels; one at the head and the other at the foot where Jesus had lain. "Woman, why weepest thou?" they asked her. "Because they have taken away my Lord," she answered, "and I know not where they have laid Him."

Then she turned away, even from the angels, thinking that she must find someone who could tell her what had been done with the body of Jesus. Another voice addressed her, "Woman, why weepest thou? whom seekest thou?" Through her tear-dimmed eyes, Mary saw the form of a man, and thinking that it was the gardener, she said, "Sir, if thou have borne Him hence, tell me where thou hast laid Him, and I will take Him away." . . .

But now in His own familiar voice Jesus said to her, "Mary." Now she knew that it was not a stranger who was addressing her, and turning she saw before her the living Christ. In her joy she forgot that He had been crucified. Springing toward Him, as if to embrace His feet, she said, "Rabboni." But Christ raised His hand, saying, Detain Me not; "for I am not yet ascended to My Father." . . .

Jesus refused to receive the homage of His people until He had the assurance that His sacrifice was accepted by the Father. He ascended to the heavenly courts, and from God Himself heard the assurance that His atonement for the sins of men had been ample, that through His blood all might gain eternal life. . . .

After He had ascended to the Father, Jesus appeared to the other women, saying. "All hail. And they came and held Him by the feet, and worshiped Him. Then said Jesus unto them, Be not afraid: go tell My brethren that they go into Galilee, and there shall they see Me."—DA 789, 790, 793.

Other Post-resurrection Appearances

Late in the afternoon of the day of the resurrection, two of the disciples were on their way to Emmaus, a little town eight miles from Jerusalem. . . . They had heard the news of the morning in regard to the removal of Christ's body from the tomb, and also the report of the women who had seen the angels and had met Jesus. They were now returning to their homes. . . .

They had not advanced far on their journey when they were joined by a stranger, but they were so absorbed in their gloom and disappointment that they did not observe Him closely. They continued their conversation, expressing the thoughts of their hearts. . . . As they talked of the events that had taken place, Jesus longed to comfort them. . . . But He must first give them lessons they would never forget. . . .

Beginning at Moses . . . Christ expounded in all the Scriptures the things concerning Himself. . . . Reasoning from prophecy, Christ gave His disciples a correct idea of what He was to be in humanity. . . .

During the journey the sun had gone down. . . . As the disciples were about to enter their home, the stranger appeared as though He would continue His journey. But the disciples felt drawn to Him. . . . "Abide with us," they said. He did not seem to accept the invitation, but they pressed it upon Him, urging, "It is toward evening, and the day is far spent." Christ yielded to this entreaty and "went in to tarry with them." . . .

The simple evening meal of bread is soon prepared. It is placed before the guest, who has taken His seat at the head of the table. Now He puts forth His hands to bless the food. The disciples start back in astonishment. Their companion spreads forth His hands in exactly the same way as their Master used to do. They look again, and lo, they see in His hands the print of nails. Both exclaim at once, It is the Lord Jesus! He has risen from the dead!

They rise to cast themselves at His feet and worship Him, but He has vanished out of their sight. . . . With this great news to communicate they cannot sit and talk. . . . They leave their meal untasted, and full of joy immediately set out again on the same path by which they came, hurrying to tell the tidings to the disciples in the city.—DA 795-801.

On reaching Jerusalem the two disciples enter at the eastern gate, which is open at night on festal occasions. . . . They go to the upper chamber where

Jesus spent the hours of the last evening before His death. . . . They find the door of the chamber securely barred. They knock for admission, but no answer comes. All is still. Then they give their names. The door is carefully unbarred, they enter, and Another, unseen, enters with them. Then the door is again fastened, to keep out spies.

The travelers find all in surprised excitement. The voices of those in the room break out into thanksgiving and praise, saying, "The Lord is risen indeed, and hath appeared to Simon." Then the two travelers . . . tell the wondrous story of how Jesus has appeared to them. They have just ended, . . . when behold, another Person stands before them. . . . Then they hear a voice which is no other than the voice of their Master. . . .

"But they were terrified and affrighted, and supposed that they had seen a spirit. And He said unto them, Why are ye troubled? and why do thoughts arise in your hearts? Behold My hands and My feet, that it is I Myself: handle Me, and see; for a spirit hath not flesh and bones, as ye see Me have. And when He had thus spoken, He showed them His hands and His feet."—DA 802, 803.

A number of the disciples now made the familiar upper chamber their temporary home, and at evening all except Thomas gathered here. One evening Thomas determined to meet with the others. . . . While the disciples were taking their evening meal, they talked of the evidences which Christ had given them in the prophecies. "Then came Jesus, the doors being shut, and stood in the midst, and said, Peace be unto you."

Turning to Thomas He said, "Reach hither thy finger, and behold My hands; and reach hither thy hand, and thrust it into My side: and be not faithless, but believing." . . . [Thomas] had no desire for further proof. His heart leaped for joy, and he cast himself at the feet of Jesus crying, "My Lord and my God."—DA 807.

Jesus had appointed to meet His disciples in Galilee; and soon after the Passover week was ended, they bent their steps thither. . . . Seven of the disciples were in company. They were clad in the humble garb of fishermen. . . . All night they toiled, without success. . . . All the while a lone watcher upon the shore followed them with His eye, while He Himself was unseen. At length the morning dawned . . . and the disciples saw a stranger standing upon the beach. . . . John recognized the stranger, and exclaimed to Peter, "It is the Lord."—DA 809, 810.

At the meeting on a mountain in Galilee, all the believers who could be called together were assembled. . . . At the time appointed, about five hundred believers were collected in little knots on the mountainside, eager to learn all that could be learned from those who had seen Christ since His resurrection. . . . Suddenly Jesus stood among them. No one could tell whence or how He came. . . . Now He declared that "all power" was given to Him. His words carried the minds of His hearers above earthly and temporal things to the heavenly and eternal.—DA 818, 819.

For forty days Christ remained on the earth, preparing the disciples for the work before them and explaining that which heretofore they had been unable to comprehend. He spoke of the prophecies concerning His advent, His rejection by the Jews, and His death, showing that every specification of these prophecies had been fulfilled. He told them that they were to regard this fulfillment of prophecy as an assurance of the power that would attend them in their future labors.—AA 26.

Christ's Final Appearance at His Ascension

The time had come for Christ to ascend to His Father's throne. . . . As the place of His ascension, Jesus chose the spot so often hallowed by His presence . . . the Mount of Olives. . . .

Now with the eleven disciples Jesus made His way toward the mountain. As they passed through the gate of Jerusalem, many wondering eyes looked upon the little company, led by One whom a few weeks before the rulers had condemned and crucified. . . .Upon reaching the Mount of Olives, Jesus led the way across the summit, to the vicinity of Bethany. Here He paused, and the disciples gathered about Him. Beams of light seemed to radiate from His countenance as He looked lovingly upon them. . . . With hands outstretched in blessing, and as if in assurance of His protecting care, He slowly ascended from among them, drawn heavenward by a power stronger than any earthly attraction. As He passed upward, the awe-stricken disciples looked with straining eyes for the last glimpse of their ascending Lord.—DA 829-831.

When Jesus . . . ascended from the Mount of Olivet, He was not only in sight of a few disciples, but many were looking on. There was a multitude of angels, thousands upon thousands who beheld the Son of God as He ascended on high.—*The Ellen G. White 1888 Materials,* 1:127.

While the disciples were still gazing upward, voices addressed them which sounded like richest music. They turned, and saw two angels in the form of men, who spoke to them, saying, "Ye men of Galilee, why stand ye gazing up into heaven? this same Jesus, which is taken up from you into heaven, shall so come in like manner as ye have seen Him go into heaven."

These angels were of the company that had been waiting in a shining cloud to escort Jesus to His heavenly home. The most exalted of the angel throng, they were the two who had come to the tomb at Christ's resurrection, and they had been with Him throughout His life on earth.—DA 831, 832.

Christ was taken up into heaven in a cloud composed of living angels.—17MR 2.

As the chariot of angels received Him, His words had come to them [the disciples], "Lo, I am with you alway, even unto the end."—AA 65.

Thousands and thousands of angels escorted Christ in honor to the city of God, singing, "Lift up your heads, O ye gates; and be ye lifted up, ye everlasting doors; and the King of glory shall come in." The angel sentinels at the gate exclaimed, "Who is this King of glory?" —RH July 29, 1890.

As He [Christ] approached the City of God . . . [the] voices [of thousands of angels] were raised and the highest angels sang, "Lift up your heads, O ye gates; and be ye lifted up, ye everlasting doors; and the King of glory shall come in."—*Ellen G. White 1888 Materials,* 1:127.

Again the challenge rings forth, "Who is this King of glory?" and the escorting angels answer, "The Lord of hosts, He is the King of glory," and the heavenly train passes through the gates.—RH July 29, 1890.

When Christ ascended up on high, and led a multitude of captives, escorted by the heavenly host, and was received in through the gates of the city, . . . He possessed the same exalted stature that He had before He came into the world to die for man.—4aSG 119.

Christ Is Escorted Into the Father's Presence

There is the throne, and around it the rainbow of promise. There are seraphim and cherubim. The angels circle round Him, but Christ waves them back. He enters into the presence of His Father. He points to His triumph . . . —those raised with Him, the representatives of the captive dead who shall come forth from their graves when the trump shall sound. He approaches the Father; and . . . says: Father, it is finished. I have done thy will, O my God. I have completed the work of redemption. If thy justice is satisfied, "I will that they also, whom thou hast given Me, be with Me where I am."—YI Aug. 11, 1898.

The arms of the Father encircle the Son, and His voice is heard, saying, "Let all the angels worship Him."—1SM 306.

The angelic throng . . . bow in adoration before Him, saying, "Worthy, worthy, is the Lamb that was slain, and lives again, a triumphant conqueror."—ST June 17, 1889.

When Christ passed within the heavenly gates, He was enthroned amidst the adoration of the angels. As soon as this ceremony was completed, the Holy Spirit descended upon the disciples in rich currents, and Christ was indeed glorified, even with the glory which He had with the Father from all eternity. The Pentecostal outpouring was Heaven's communication that the Redeemer's inauguration was accomplished. According to His promise He had sent the Holy Spirit from heaven to His followers, as a token that He had, as Priest and King, received all authority in heaven and on earth, and was the Anointed One over His people. —AA 38.

18.

Angels From Pentecost to the Last Days

Angels Protect Vital Truths

I saw the angels of God were commissioned to guard with special care the sacred, important truths which were to serve as an anchor to the disciples of Christ through every generation. The Holy Spirit especially rested upon the apostles, who were witnesses of our Lord's crucifixion, resurrection, and ascension—important truths which were to be the hope of Israel. All were to look to the Saviour of the world as their only hope, and walk in the way which He had opened by the sacrifice of His own life, and keep God's law and live. I saw the wisdom and goodness of Jesus in giving power to the disciples to carry on the same work for which He had been hated and slain by the Jews. In His name they had power over the works of Satan. A halo of light and glory centered about the time of Jesus' death and resurrection, immortalizing the sacred truth that He was the Saviour of the world. —EW 196, 197.

Peter and John Delivered From Prison

A short time after the descent of the Holy Spirit, and immediately after a season of fervent prayer, Peter and John, going up to the temple to worship, saw a distressed and poverty-stricken cripple. . . . The disciples regarded him with compassion. "And Peter, fastening his eyes upon him with John, said, Look on us." "Silver and gold have I none; but such as I have give I thee. In the name of Jesus Christ of Nazareth rise up and walk."—3SP 275, 276.

As the Sadducees, who did not believe in a resurrection, heard the apostles declaring that Christ had risen from the dead, they were enraged, realizing that if the apostles were allowed to preach a risen Saviour, and to work miracles in His name, the doctrine that there would be no resurrection would be rejected by all, and the sect of the Sadducees would soon become extinct.—AA 78.

Some of the officials of the temple, and the captain of the temple, were Sadducees. The captain, with the help of a number of Sadducees, arrested the two apostles, and put them in prison, as it was too late for their cases to be examined that night.—3SP 278.

Satan triumphed, and the evil angels exulted; but the angels of God were sent and opened the prison doors, and, contrary to the command of the high priest and elders, bade them go into the temple, and speak all the words of this life.—1SG 83, 84.

In the meantime the high priest and those with him had "called the council together, and all the senate of the children of Israel." The priests and rulers had decided to fix upon the disciples the charge of insurrection, to accuse them of murdering Ananias and Sapphira, and of conspiring to deprive the priests of their authority.

When they sent for the prisoners to be brought before them, great was their amazement at the word brought back, that the prison doors were found to be securely bolted, and the guard stationed before them, but that the prisoners were nowhere to be found.

Soon the astonishing report came, "Behold, the men whom ye put in prison are standing in the temple, and teaching the people. Then went the captain with the officers, and brought them without violence: for they feared the people, lest they should have been stoned."

As they [Peter and John] stood for the second time before the men who seemed bent on their destruction, no fear or hesitation could be discerned in their words or attitude. And when the high priest said, "Did we not straitly command you that ye should not teach in this name? and, behold, ye have filled Jerusalem with your doctrine, and intend to bring this man's blood upon us," Peter answered, "We ought to obey God rather than men." It was an angel from heaven who delivered them from prison and bade them teach in the temple.—AA 78-82.

Then were those murderers enraged. They wished to imbrue their hands in blood again by slaying the apostles. They were planning how to do this, when an angel from God was sent to Gamaliel to move upon his heart to counsel the chief priests and rulers. Said Gamaliel, Refrain from these men, and let them alone; for if this counsel or this work be of men, it will come to naught; but if it be of God ye cannot overthrow it; lest haply ye be found even to fight against God.

The evil angels were moving upon the priests and elders to put the apostles to death; but God sent His angel to prevent it, by raising up a voice in favor of the disciples in their own ranks.—1SG 85.

Philip and the Ethiopian Eunuch

Heavenly angels watch those who are seeking for enlightenment. They cooperate with those who try to win souls to Christ. Angels minister to those who shall be heirs of salvation. This is shown in the experience of Philip and the Ethiopian.—BE&ST Dec. 10, 1900.

This Ethiopian was a man of good standing and of wide influence. God saw that when converted he would give others the light he had received and would exert a strong influence in favor of the gospel. Angels of God were attending this seeker for light, and he was being drawn to the Saviour. By the ministration of the Holy Spirit the Lord brought him into touch with one who would lead him to the light.—CC 332.

When God pointed out to Philip his work, . . . he learned that every soul is precious in the sight of God, and that angels will bring to the appointed agencies light for those who are in need of it. The heavenly angels do not undertake the work of preaching the gospel. Through the ministration of angels God sends light to His people, and through His people this light is to be given to the world.—BE&ST Dec. 10, 1900.

Paul's Conversion

As Saul journeyed to Damascus, with letters authorizing him to take men or women who were preaching Jesus, and bring them bound to Jerusalem, evil angels exulted around him. But suddenly a light from heaven shone round about him, which made the evil angels flee.—EW 200.

In the record of the conversion of Saul, important principles are given us, which we should ever bear in mind. Saul was brought directly into the presence of Christ. . . . He arrested him in his course and convicted him of sin; but when Saul asked, "What wilt Thou have me to do?" the Saviour placed the inquiring Jew in connection with His church, there to obtain a knowledge of God's will concerning him. . . .

While Saul in solitude at the house of Judas continued in prayer and supplication, the Lord appeared in vision to "a certain disciple at Damascus, named Ananias," telling him that Saul of Tarsus was praying, and in need of help. "Arise, and go into the street which is called Straight," the heavenly messenger said, "and inquire in the house of Judas for one called Saul, of Tarsus: for, behold, he prayeth." . . .

Ananias could scarcely credit the words of the angel; for the reports of Saul's bitter persecution of the saints at Jerusalem had spread far and wide. . . .

Obedient to the direction of the angel, Ananias sought out the man who had but recently breathed out threatenings against all who believed on the name of Jesus; and putting his hands on the head of the penitent sufferer, he said, "Brother Saul, the Lord, even Jesus, that appeared unto thee in the way as thou camest, hath sent me, that thou mightest receive thy sight, and be filled with the Holy Ghost.

"And immediately there fell from his eyes as it had been scales: and he received sight forthwith, and arose, and was baptized."—AA 120-122.

Paul Leaves Damascus

As Paul preached Christ in Damascus, all who heard him were amazed. . . . The opposition grew so fierce that Paul was not allowed to continue his labors at Damascus. A messenger from heaven bade him leave for a time; and he "went into Arabia" (Gal. 1:17), where he found a safe retreat.

Here, in the solitude of the desert, Paul had ample opportunity for quiet study and meditation. . . . Jesus communed with him, and established him in the faith, bestowing upon him a rich measure of wisdom and grace.—AA 124-126.

Paul's labors at Antioch, in association with Barnabas, strengthened him in his conviction that the Lord had called him to do a special work for the Gentile world. At the time of Paul's conversion, the Lord had declared that he was to be made a minister to the

Gentiles, "to open their eyes, and to turn them from darkness to light, and from the power of Satan unto God, that they may receive the forgiveness of sins, and inheritance among them which are sanctified by faith that is in Me." Acts 26:18. The angel that appeared to Ananias, had said of Paul, "He is a chosen vessel unto Me, to bear My name before the Gentiles, and kings, and the children of Israel." Acts 9:15. And Paul himself, later in his Christian experience, while praying in the temple at Jerusalem, had been visited by an angel from heaven, who bade him, "Depart: for I will send thee far hence unto the Gentiles." Acts 22:21.—AA 159.

Cornelius and Peter

The same Holy Watcher who said of Abraham, "I know him," knew Cornelius also, and sent a message direct from heaven to him.—AA 133.

The angel appeared to Cornelius while he was at prayer. As the centurion heard himself addressed by name, he was afraid, yet he knew that the messenger had come from God, and he said, "What is it, Lord?" —AA 133.

"Send men for one Simon, whose surname is Peter, who lives with one Simon a tanner." And he told him the very place where Simon the tanner lived. Then the angel of the Lord went to Peter, and prepared his mind for the reception of the men.—*Ellen G. White 1888 Materials*, 1746.

Cornelius was gladly obedient to the vision. When the angel had gone, he called "two of his household servants, and a devout soldier of them that waited on him continually; and when he had declared all these things unto them, he sent them to Joppa.". . . The angel was not commissioned to tell Cornelius the story of the cross. A man subject even as the centurion himself to human frailties and temptations was to tell him of the crucified and risen Saviour. In His wisdom the Lord brings those who are seeking for truth into touch with fellow beings who know the truth.—RH April 6, 1911.

Immediately after the interview with Cornelius, the angel went to Peter, who, at the time, was praying upon the housetop of his lodging in Joppa.—RH April 13, 1911.

It was with reluctance at every step that Peter undertook the duty laid upon him by divine command. When relating his experience, he does not defend his action on general principles, but as an exception, done because of divine revelation. And the result was a surprise to him. When Cornelius had related to him his experience, and the words of the angel who had appeared to him in vision, Peter declared, "Of a truth I perceive that God is no respecter of persons; but in every nation he that feareth Him, and worketh righteousness, is accepted with Him."—6MR 328, 329.

Peter Delivered From Prison

The day of Peter's execution was at last appointed;

but still the prayers of the believers ascended to Heaven. And while all their energies and sympathies were called out in fervent appeals, angels of God were guarding the imprisoned apostle. . . . Peter was placed between two soldiers, and was bound by two chains, each chain being fastened to the wrist of one of his guard. He was therefore unable to move without their knowledge. The prison doors were securely fastened, and a strong guard was placed before them. All chance of rescue or escape, by human means, was thus cut off. —*Redemption: or the Ministry of Peter and the Conversion of Saul* 70.

Peter was in prison, expecting to be brought forth next day to death; he was sleeping at night "between two soldiers, bound with two chains: and the keepers before the door kept the prison. And, behold, the angel of the Lord came upon him, and a light shined in the prison: and he smote Peter on the side, and raised him up, saying, Arise up quickly. And his chains fell off from his hands."

Peter, suddenly awaking, was amazed at the brightness that flooded his dungeon, and the celestial beauty of the heavenly messenger. He understood not the scene, but he knew that he was free, and in his bewilderment and joy he would have gone forth from the prison unprotected from the cold night air. The angel of God, noting all the circumstances, said, with tender care for the apostle's need: "Gird thyself, and bind on thy sandals."

Peter mechanically obeyed; but so entranced was he with the revelation of the glory of heaven that he did not think to take his cloak. Then the angel bade him: "Cast thy garment about thee, and follow me. And he went out, and followed him; and wist not that it was true which was done by the angel; but thought he saw a vision. When they were past the first and the second ward, they came unto the iron gate that leadeth unto the city; which opened to them of his own accord."—5T 748.

No word is spoken; there is no sound of footsteps. The angel glides on in front, encircled by a light of dazzling brightness, and Peter, bewildered, and still believing himself to be in a dream, follows his deliverer. Thus they pass on through one street, and then, the mission of the angel being accomplished, he suddenly disappears.

The heavenly light faded away, and Peter felt himself to be in profound darkness; but as his eyes became accustomed to the darkness, it gradually seemed to lessen, and he found himself alone in the silent street, with the cool night air blowing upon his brow. He now realized that he was free, in a familiar part of the city; he recognized the place as one that he had often frequented, and had expected to pass on the morrow for the last time. . . .

The apostle made his way at once to the house where his brethren were assembled, and where they were at that moment engaged in earnest prayer for him. "As Peter knocked at the door of the gate, a damsel came to hearken, named Rhoda. And when she knew Peter's voice, she opened not the gate for gladness, but ran in, and told how Peter stood before the gate. And they said unto her, Thou art mad. But she constantly affirmed that it was even so. Then said they, It is his angel." —AA 147, 148.

The same angel who had left the royal courts of heaven to rescue Peter from the power of his persecutor, had been the messenger of wrath and judgment to Herod. The angel smote Peter to arouse him from slumber; but it was with a different stroke that he smote the wicked king, bringing mortal disease upon him. —3SP 344.

The Stoning of Stephen

As he [Stephen] looked up steadfastly into heaven, a vision of God's glory was given him, and angels hovered around him. He cried out, Behold, I see the heavens opened, and the Son of man standing on the right hand of God.—1SG 89.

Angels During Paul's Ministry

An extensive and profitable business had grown up at Ephesus from the manufacture and sale of small shrines and images, modeled after the temple and the image of Diana. Those interested in this industry found their gains diminishing, and all united in attributing the unwelcome change to Paul's labors. . . .

"The whole city was filled with confusion." Search was made for Paul, but the apostle was not to be found. His brethren, receiving an intimation of the danger, had hurried him out of the place. Angels of God had been sent to guard the apostle; his time to die a martyr's death had not yet come.—AA 292, 293.

Day after day, as they [Paul and Silas] went to their devotions [in Philippi], a woman with the spirit of divination followed them, crying, "These men are the servants of the most high God, which show unto us the way of salvation." This woman was a special agent of Satan; and, as the devils were troubled by the presence of Christ, so the evil spirit which possessed her was ill at ease in the presence of the apostles. Satan knew that his kingdom was invaded, and took this way of opposing the work of the ministers of God. The words of recommendation uttered by this woman were an injury to the cause, distracting the minds of the people from the truths presented to them, and throwing disrepute upon the work by causing people to believe that the men who spoke with the Spirit and power of God were actuated by the same spirit as this emissary of Satan.

The apostles endured this opposition for several days; then Paul, under inspiration of the Spirit of God, commanded the evil spirit to leave the woman. Satan was thus met and rebuked. The immediate and continued silence of the woman testified that the apostles were the servants of God, and that the demon had acknowledged them to be such, and had obeyed their command. When the woman was dispossessed of the spirit of the devil, and restored to herself, her masters were alarmed for their craft. They saw that all hope of receiving money from her divinations and soothsayings was at an end, and perceived that, if the apostles were allowed to continue their work, their own source of income would soon be entirely cut off.—LP 74, 75.

After the woman had been freed from the evil spirit, she became a follower of Christ. Her masters saw that their hope of gain was gone, and taking Paul and Silas, they brought them before the rulers, charging them with troubling the city. This caused an uproar. The multitude rose against the disciples, and the magistrates commanded that the prisoners should be beaten.—RH June 29, 1905.

When they [the magistrates] had laid many stripes upon them [Paul and Silas], they cast them into prison, charging the jailer to keep them safely, who, having received such a charge, thrust them into the inner prison and made their feet fast in the stocks. But the angels of God accompanied them within the prison walls.—1SG 95, 96.

The apostles suffered extreme torture because of the painful position in which they were left, but they did not murmur. Instead, in the utter darkness and desolation of the dungeon, they encouraged each other by words of prayer, and sang praises to God because they were found worthy to suffer shame for His sake. . . . With astonishment the other prisoners heard the sound of prayer and singing issuing from the inner prison. —AA 213, 214.

While men were cruel and vindictive, or criminally negligent of the solemn responsibilities devolving upon them, God had not forgotten to be gracious to His suffering servants. An angel was sent from heaven to release the apostles. As he neared the Roman prison, the earth trembled beneath his feet, the whole city was shaken by the earthquake, and the prison walls reeled like a reed in the wind. The heavily bolted doors flew open; the chains and fetters fell from the hands and feet of every prisoner.—3SP 382, 383.

The apostle Paul, in his labors at Ephesus, was given special tokens of divine favor. The power of God accompanied his efforts, and many were healed of physical maladies. "God wrought special miracles by the hands of Paul: so that from his body were brought unto the sick handkerchiefs or aprons, and the diseases departed from them, and the evil spirits went out of them."

These manifestations of supernatural power were far more potent than had ever before been witnessed in Ephesus, and were of such a character that they could not be imitated by the skill of the juggler or the enchantments of the sorcerer. As these miracles were wrought in the name of Jesus of Nazareth, the people had opportunity to see that the God of heaven was more powerful than the magicians who were worshipers of the goddess Diana. Thus the Lord exalted His servant, even before the idolaters themselves, immeasurably above the most powerful and favored of the magicians.

But the One to whom all the spirits of evil are subject and who had given His servants authority over them, was about to bring still greater shame and defeat upon those who despised and profaned His holy name. Sorcery had been prohibited by the Mosaic law, on pain of death, yet from time to time it had been secretly practiced by apostate Jews. At the time of Paul's visit to Ephesus, there were in the city "certain of the vagabond Jews, exorcists," who, seeing the wonders wrought by him [Paul], "took upon them to call over them which had evil spirits the name of the Lord Jesus." An attempt was made by "seven sons of one Sceva, a Jew, and chief of the priests." Finding a man possessed with a demon, they addressed him, "We adjure you by Jesus whom Paul preacheth." But "the evil spirit answered and said, Jesus I know, and Paul I know; but who are ye? And the man in whom the evil spirit was leaped on them, and overcame them, and prevailed against them, so that they fled out of that house naked and wounded.". . .

Facts which had previously been concealed were now brought to light. In accepting Christianity some of the believers had not fully renounced their superstitions. To some extent they still continued the practice of magic. Now, convinced of their error, "many that believed came, and confessed, and showed their deeds." Even to some of the sorcerers themselves the good work extended; and "many of them also which used curious arts brought their books together, and burned them before all men." . . .

These treatises on divination contained rules and forms of communication with evil spirits. They were the regulations of the worship of Satan—directions for soliciting his help and obtaining information from him.—AA 286-289.

A report of the speech of Demetrius was rapidly circulated. The uproar was terrific. The whole city [of

Ephesus] seemed in commotion. An immense crowd soon collected, and a rush was made to the workshop of Aquila, in the Jewish quarters, with the object of securing Paul. In their insane rage they were ready to tear him in pieces. But the apostle was not to be found. His brethren, receiving an intimation of the danger, had hurried him from the place. Angels of God were sent to guard the faithful apostle.—LP 143.

As the chief priests and rulers witnessed the effect of the relation of Paul's experience, they were moved with hatred against him. They saw that he boldly preached Jesus and wrought miracles in His name, that multitudes listened to him and turned from their traditions and looked upon the Jewish leaders as the murderers of the Son of God. Their anger was kindled, and they assembled to consult as to what was best to be done to put down the excitement. They agreed that the only safe course was to put Paul to death. But God knew of their intention, and angels were commissioned to guard him, that he might live to fulfill his mission.—EW 202.

This portion of history has been written for our admonition, upon whom the ends of the world are come. The Ephesians claimed to have interaction with invisible beings, from whom they derived their knowledge of that which was to come to pass. In our day this communion with spirits is called Spiritualism, and the arts practiced by mediums are not all sleight of hand, cunning, and pretense. The visible and invisible worlds are in close connection. Satan is the master deceiver, and his confederates in evil are in training under him to work in the same line in which he works. The apostle says, "We wrestle not against flesh and blood, but against principalities, against powers, against the rulers of the darkness of this world, against spiritual wickedness in high places. Wherefore take unto you the whole armor of God, that ye may be able to withstand in the evil day."—YI Nov. 16, 1893.

That aged prisoner [Paul], standing chained to his soldier guard, presented nothing imposing or attractive in his dress or appearance, that the world should pay him homage. Yet this man, apparently without friends or wealth or position, had an escort that worldlings could not see. Angels of heaven were his attendants. Had the glory of one of those shining messengers flashed forth, the pomp and pride of royalty would have paled before it; king and courtiers would have been stricken to the earth. . . . All heaven was interested in this one man, now held a prisoner for his faith in the Son of God.—LP 254.

The Siege of Jerusalem

The longsuffering of God toward Jerusalem only confirmed the Jews in their stubborn impenitence. In their hatred and cruelty toward the disciples of Jesus, they rejected the last offer of mercy. Then God withdrew His protection from them, and removed His restraining power from Satan and his angels, and the nation was left to the control of the leader she had chosen. Her children had spurned the grace of Christ, which would have enabled them to subdue their evil impulses, and now these became the conquerors.

Satan aroused the fiercest and most debased passions of the soul. Men did not reason; they were beyond reason—controlled by impulse and blind rage. They became satanic in their cruelty. . . . Satan was at the head of the nation, and the highest civil and religious authorities were under his sway.—4SP 29, 30.

Angels of God were sent to do the work of destruction, so that one stone [of the temple] was not left upon another that was not thrown down.—21MR 66.

John the Revelator

Of Gabriel the Saviour speaks in the Revelation, saying that "He sent and signified it by His angel unto His servant John." Rev. 1:1. And to John the angel declared, "I am a fellow servant with thee and with thy brethren the prophets." Rev. 22:9, R.V. Wonderful thought—that the angel who stands next in honor to the Son of God is the one chosen to open the purposes of God to sinful men.—DA 99.

God had a special work for him to accomplish. Satan was determined to hinder this work, and he led on his servants to destroy John. But God sent His angel and wonderfully preserved him. All who witnessed the great power of God manifested in the deliverance of John, were astonished, and many were convinced that God was with him, and that the testimony which he bore concerning Jesus was correct. Those who sought to destroy him were afraid to again attempt to take his life, and he was permitted to suffer on for Jesus.

He was falsely accused by his enemies, and was shortly banished to a lonely island, where the Lord sent His angel to reveal to him things which were to take place upon the earth, and the state of the church down through to the end; her backslidings, and the position the church should occupy if she would please God, and finally overcome.

The angel from heaven came to John in majesty. His countenance beamed with the excellent glory of heaven. He revealed to John scenes of deep and thrilling interest concerning the church of God, and brought before him the perilous conflicts they were to endure. John saw them pass through fiery trials, and made white and tried, and, finally, victorious overcomers, gloriously saved in the kingdom of God. The countenance of the angel grew radiant with joy, and was exceeding glorious, as he showed to John the final triumph of the church of God.

John was enraptured as he beheld the final deliverance of the church, and as he was carried away with the glory of the scene, with deep reverence and awe he fell at the feet of the angel to worship him. The angel instantly raised him up, and gently reproved him, saying, See thou do it not; I am thy fellow servant, and of thy brethren that have the testimony of Jesus; worship God; for the testimony of Jesus is the spirit of prophecy.

The angel then showed John the heavenly city with all its splendor and dazzling glory. John was enraptured and overwhelmed with the glory of the city. He did not bear in mind his former reproof from the angel, but again fell to worship before the feet of the angel, who again gave the gentle reproof, See thou do it not; for I am thy fellow servant, and of thy brethren the prophets, and of them that keep the sayings of this book; worship God.—1SG 130, 131.

Christ, the royal messenger, came to John when on his sea-bound isle, and gave him the most wonderful revelations of Himself.—ST March 3, 1890.

The mighty Angel [of Revelation 10] who instructed John was no less a personage than Jesus Christ. Setting His right foot on the sea, and His left upon the dry land, shows the part which He is acting in the closing scenes of the great controversy with Satan. This position denotes His supreme power and authority over the whole earth. The controversy has waxed stronger and more determined from age to age, and will continue to do so, to the concluding scenes when the masterly working of the powers of darkness shall reach their height. Satan, united with evil men, will deceive the whole world and the churches who receive not the love of the truth. But the mighty Angel demands attention. He cries with a loud voice. He is to show the power and authority of His voice to those who have united with Satan to oppose the truth.—7BC 971.

Angels in the Middle Ages

In the thirteenth century was established that most

terrible of all the engines of the papacy—the Inquisition. The prince of darkness wrought with the leaders of the papal hierarchy. In their secret councils, Satan and his angels controlled the minds of evil men, while unseen in the midst stood an angel of God, taking the fearful record of their iniquitous decrees and writing the history of deeds too horrible to appear to human eyes.—GC 59.

The Protestant Reformation

The banner of the ruler of the synagogue of Satan was lifted high, and error apparently marched in triumph, and the reformers, through the grace given them of God, waged a successful warfare against the hosts of darkness. Events in the history of the reformers have been presented before me. I know that the Lord Jesus and His angels have with intense interest watched the battle against the power of Satan, who combined his hosts with evil men, for the purpose of extinguishing the divine light.—3SM 110.

Luther

While one day examining the books in the library of the university, Luther discovered a Latin Bible. . . . With mingled awe and wonder he turned the sacred pages; with quickened pulse and throbbing heart he read for himself the words of life, pausing now and then to exclaim, "Oh, if God would give me such a book for my own!" Angels of heaven were by his side, and rays of light from the throne of God revealed the treasures of truth to his understanding.—4SP 96.

When enemies appealed to custom and tradition, or to the assertions and authority of the pope, Luther met them with the Bible and the Bible alone. Here were arguments which they could not answer; therefore the slaves of formalism and superstition clamored for his blood. . . . But Luther did not fall a prey to their fury. God had a work for him to do, and angels of heaven were sent to protect him.—4SP 108, 109.

Here was one lone man who had stirred the rage of priests and people. He was summoned to Augsburg to answer for his faith. He obeyed the summons. Firm and undaunted he stood before those who had caused the world to tremble—a meek lamb surrounded by angry lions—yet for the truth's sake, and for Christ's sake, he stood up undaunted, and with holy eloquence, which the truth can alone inspire, he gave the reasons of his faith. They tried various means to silence the bold advocate for truth. They flattered and held out inducements; he should be exalted and honored; but life and honors were valueless to him, if purchased at the sacrifice of the truth.

Brighter and clearer shone the Word of God upon his understanding, giving him a more vivid sense of the errors, corruptions, and hypocrisy of the papacy. His enemies sought to intimidate him, and cause him to renounce his faith, but he boldly stood in defense of the truth. He was ready to die for his faith, if God required; but to yield it—never. God preserved his life. He bade angels attend him, and bring him through the

stormy conflict, unharmed, and he baffled the rage and
purposes of his enemies.—4bSG 118, 119.

Had the eyes of the assembly [at Worms] been
opened, they would have beheld angels of God in the
midst of them, shedding beams of light athwart the
darkness of error, and opening minds and hearts to the
reception of truth.—4SP 124.

Melancthon

[The Reformer, Simon] Grynaeus had been on intimate terms with a leading papist doctor; but, having
been shocked at one of his sermons, he went to him, and
entreated that he would no longer war against the truth.
The papist concealed his anger, but immediately repaired
to the king, and obtained from him authority to arrest
the protester. When Melancthon returned to his house,
he was informed that after his departure officers in pur-
suit of Grynaeus had searched it from top to bottom. He
ever believed that the Lord had saved his friend by sending a holy angel to give him warning.—4SP 164, 165.

The Pilgrim Fathers

In the midst of exile and hardship their [the Pilgrim
fathers] love and faith waxed strong. They trusted the
Lord's promises, and He did not fail them in time of need.
His angels were by their side, to encourage and support
them. And when God's hand seemed pointing them
across the sea, to a land where they might found for
themselves a state, and leave to their children the pre-

cious heritage of religious liberty, they went forward, without shrinking, in the path of providence.—GC 291.

The Three Angels of Revelation 14

Christ is coming the second time, with power unto salvation. To prepare human beings for this event, He has sent the first, second, and third angels' messages. These angels represent those who receive the truth, and with power open the gospel to the world.—7BC 978, 979.

William Miller

I saw that God sent His angel to move upon the heart of a farmer [William Miller] who had not believed the Bible, and led him to search the prophecies. Angels of God repeatedly visited that chosen one, and guided his mind, and opened his understanding to prophecies which had ever been dark to God's people. The commencement of the chain of truth was given him, and he was led on to search for link after link, until he looked with wonder and admiration upon the Word of God. . . .

Angels of God accompanied William Miller in his mission. He was firm and undaunted. He fearlessly proclaimed the message. . . . Although opposed by professed Christians and the world, and buffeted by Satan and his angels, he ceased not to preach the everlasting gospel to crowds wherever he was invited, and sound the cry, Fear God and give glory to Him; for the hour of His judgment is come.—1SG 128, 132.

The instigator of all evil sought not only to counteract the effect of the advent message, but to destroy the messenger himself. Miller made a practical application of Scripture truth to the hearts of his hearers, reproving their sins and disturbing their self-satisfaction, and his plain and cutting words aroused their enmity. The opposition manifested by church members toward his message emboldened the baser classes to go to greater lengths; and enemies plotted to take his life as he should leave the place of meeting. But holy angels were in the throng, and one of these, in the form of a man, took the arm of this servant of the Lord, and led him in safety from the angry mob.—GC 336, 337.

Many ministers would not accept this saving message themselves, and those who would receive it, they hindered. The blood of souls is upon them. Preachers and people joined to oppose this message from heaven. They persecuted William Miller and those who united with him in the work. Falsehoods were circulated to injure his influence, and at different times after he had plainly declared the counsel of God, applying cutting truths to the hearts of his hearers, great rage was kindled against him, and as he left the place of meeting, some waylaid him in order to take his life. But angels of God were sent to preserve his life, and they led him safely away from the angry mob.—1SG 136.

19.

Angels in Ellen White's Experience

Ellen White's Call to Be a Prophet

While I was praying at the family altar, the Holy Ghost fell upon me, and I seemed to be rising higher and higher, far above the dark world. I turned to look for the Advent people in the world, but could not find them, when a voice said to me, "Look again, and look a little higher." At this I raised my eyes, and saw a straight and narrow path, cast up high above the world. On this path the Advent people were traveling to the city, which was at the farther end of the path. They had a bright light set up behind them at the beginning of the path, which an angel told me was the midnight cry. This light shone all the way along the path and gave light for their feet so that they might not stumble. If they kept their eyes fixed on Jesus, who was just before them, leading them to the city, they were safe. —EW 14.

At the age of seventeen . . . a heavenly visitant came and spoke to me, saying, "I have a message for you to bear." "Why," I thought, "there certainly must be a great mistake somewhere." Again were spoken the words: "I have a message for you to bear. Write out for the people what I have given you."—2SAT 252.

The Ark of the Covenant in Heaven

The Lord gave me a view of the heavenly sanctuary. The temple of God was opened in heaven, and I was shown the ark of God covered with the mercy-seat. Two angels stood at either end of the ark, with their wings spread over the mercy-seat, and their faces turned toward it. This my accompanying angel informed me represented all the heavenly host looking with reverential awe toward the Law of God which had been written by the finger of God.—LS (1880) 237.

The ark of the earthly sanctuary was the pattern of the true ark in heaven. There, beside the heavenly ark, stand living angels, each with one wing overshadowing the mercy-seat, and stretching forth on high, while the other wings are folded over their forms in token of reverence and humility.—ST June 24, 1880.

Oh, that all could behold our precious Saviour as He is, *a Saviour*. Let His hand draw aside the veil which conceals His glory from our eyes. It shows Him in His high and holy place. What do we see? Our Saviour, not in a position of silence and inactivity. He is surrounded with heavenly intelligences, cherubim, and seraphim, ten thousand times ten thousand of angels.

All these heavenly beings have one object above all others, in which they are intensely interested—

His church in a world of corruption. . . . They are working for Christ under His commission, to save to the uttermost all who look to Him and believe in Him. These heavenly intelligences are speeding on their mission. . . . They are united in a holy alliance, in a grand and sublime unity of purpose, to show forth the power and compassion and love and glory of the crucified and risen Saviour.

In their service, these armies of heaven illustrate what the church of God should be. Christ is working in their behalf in the heavenly courts, sending out His messengers to all parts of the globe, to the assistance of every suffering one who looks to Him for relief, for spiritual life and knowledge.—7BC 967, 968.

Satan Before He Fell and As He Is Now

Satan was once an honored angel in heaven, next to Christ. His countenance, like those of the other angels, was mild and expressive of happiness. His forehead was high and broad, showing great intelligence. His form was perfect; his bearing noble and majestic.—EW 145.

I was shown Satan as he once was, a happy, exalted angel. Then I was shown him as he now is. He still bears a kingly form. His features are still noble, for he is an angel fallen. But the expression of his countenance is full of anxiety, care, unhappiness, malice, hate, mischief, deceit, and every evil. That brow which was once so noble, I particularly noticed. His forehead commenced from his eyes to recede. I saw that he had so long bent himself to evil that every good quality was debased, and every evil trait was developed. His eyes were cunning, sly, and showed great penetration. His frame was large, but the flesh hung loosely about his hands and face. As I beheld him, his chin was resting upon his left hand. He appeared to be in deep thought. A smile was upon his countenance, which made me tremble, it was so full of evil and satanic slyness. This smile is the one he wears just before he makes sure of his victim, and as he fastens the victim in his snare, this smile grows horrible.—EW 152, 153.

Angels Ellen White Saw in Visions and Dreams

I dreamed that several of the brethren in California were in council, considering the best plan for labor during the coming season. Some thought it wise to shun the large cities, and work in smaller places. My husband was earnestly urging that broader plans be laid, and more extended efforts made, which would better compare with the character of our message.

Then a young man whom I had frequently seen in my dreams, came into the council. He listened with deep interest to the words that were spoken, and then, speaking with deliberation and authoritative confidence, said:

"The cities and villages constitute a part of the Lord's vineyard. They must hear the messages of warning. The enemy of truth is making desperate efforts to turn the people from the truth of God to falsehood. . . . You are to sow beside all waters."—LS 208.

In my work, I am connected with my helpers, and I am also connected with and in close touch with my

Instructor and other heavenly intelligences. Those who are called of God should be in touch with Him through the operation of His Holy Spirit, that they may be taught of Him.—*Spaulding and Magan Collection* 462.

While riding in the cars I was unable to sit up. My husband made a bed on the seat, and I lay down with aching head and heart. . . .

In this state of mind I fell asleep and dreamed that a tall angel stood by my side, and asked me why I was sad. I related to him the thoughts that had troubled me, and said, "I can do so little good, why may we not be with our children, and enjoy their society?" Said he, "You have given to the Lord two beautiful flowers, the fragrance of which is as sweet incense before Him, and is more precious in His sight than gold or silver, for it is a heart gift. It draws upon every fibre of the heart as no other sacrifice can. You should not look upon present appearances, but keep the eye single to your duty, single to God's glory, and follow in His opening providence, and the path shall brighten before you. Every self-denial, every sacrifice is faithfully recorded, and will bring its reward."—2SG 129, 130.

I dreamed that a young man of noble appearance came into the room where I was, immediately after I had been speaking. This same person has appeared before me in important dreams to instruct me from time to time during the past twenty-six years. Said he, You have called the attention of the people to important subjects, which, to a large number, are strange and new. To some they are intensely interesting. The laborers in word and doctrine have done what they could in presenting the truth, which has raised inquiry in minds and awakened an interest. But unless there is a more thorough effort made to fasten these impressions upon minds, your efforts now made will prove nearly fruitless.—RH Nov. 4, 1875.

As inquiries are frequently made as to my state in vision, and after I come out, I would say that when the Lord sees fit to give a vision, I am taken into the presence of Jesus and angels, and am entirely lost to earthly things. I can see no farther than the angel directs me. —2SG 292.

The Battle of Manassas

I had a view of the disastrous battle at Manassas, Virginia. It was a most exciting, distressing scene. The Southern army had everything in their favor and were prepared for a dreadful contest. The Northern army was moving on with triumph, not doubting but that they would be victorious. Many were reckless and marched forward boastingly, as though victory were already theirs. As they neared the battlefield, many were almost fainting through weariness and want of refreshment. They did not expect so fierce an encounter. They rushed into battle and fought bravely, desperately. The dead and dying were on every side. Both the North and the South suffered severely. The Southern men felt the battle, and in a little while would have been driven back still further. The Northern men were rushing on, although their destruction was very great.

Just then an angel descended and waved his hand backward. Instantly there was confusion in the ranks. It appeared to the Northern men that their troops were retreating, when it was not so in reality, and a precipitate retreat commenced.—1T 266, 267.

The Sanitarium Manager

In my dreams I was at the Health Retreat, and I was told by my guide to mark everything I heard and to observe everything I saw. I was in a retired place, where I could not be seen, but could see all that went on in the room. Persons were settling accounts with you, and I heard them remonstrating with you in regard to the large sum charged for board and room and treatment. I heard you with firm, decided voice refuse to lower the charge. I was astonished to see that the charge was so high. You seemed to be the controlling power.

I saw that the impression made by your course on the minds of those who were settling their bills was unfavorable to the institution. I heard some of your brethren pleading with you, telling you that your course was unwise and unjust, but you were as firm as a rock in your adherence to your course. You claimed that in what you were doing, you were working for the good of the institution. But I saw persons go from the Retreat anything but satisfied. . . .

In the night season I saw you in the company of the matron of the institution. As far as your attentions to each other were concerned, you might have been man and wife. Your conduct toward each other was wrong in the sight of God, and my heart was grieved by the condition of things. I asked, "Who hath bewitched you, that ye should not obey the truth?" God is displeased. You have grieved His Holy Spirit. Sister H____ will never again be what she once was. Both of you are guilty before God. . . .

The things that transpired in . . . [the sanitarium] were opened before me. A voice said, "Follow me, and I will show you the sins that are practiced by those who stand in responsible positions." I went through the rooms, and I saw you, a watchman upon the walls of Zion, were very intimate with another man's wife, betraying sacred trusts, crucifying your Lord afresh. Did you consider that there was a Watcher, the Holy One, who was witnessing your evil work, seeing your actions and hearing your words, and these are also registered in the books of heaven?—8MR 315-317.

The Brown Family

The angel of God said, "Follow me." I seemed to be in a room in a rude building, and there were several young men playing cards. They seemed to be very intent upon the amusement in which they were engaged and were so engrossed that they did not seem to notice that anyone had entered the room. There were young girls present observing the players, and words were spoken not of the most refined order. There was a spirit and influence that were sensibly felt in that room that was not of a character calculated to purify and uplift the mind and ennoble the character. . . .

I inquired, "Who are these and what does this scene represent?"

The word was spoken, "Wait." . . .

I had another representation. There was the imbibing of the liquid poison, and the words and actions under its influence were anything but favorable for serious thoughts, clear perception in business lines, pure morals, and the uplifting of the participants. . . .

I asked again, "Who are these?"

The answer came, "A portion of the family where you are visiting. The adversary of souls, the great enemy of God and man, the head of principalities and powers, and the ruler of the darkness of this world is presiding here tonight. Satan and his angels are leading on with his temptations these poor souls to their own ruin."—3SM 41, 42.

N. D. Faulkhead and the Secret Sign

Brother Faulkhead called to see me. The burden of his case was upon my mind. I told him that I had a message for him and his wife, which I had several times prepared to send them, but I had felt forbidden by the Spirit of the Lord to do so. I asked him to appoint a time when I could see them. He answered, "I am glad that you did not send me a written communication; I would rather have the message from your lips; had it come in another way I do not think it would have done me any good." He then asked, "Why not give me the message now?" I said, "Can you remain to hear it?" He replied that he would do so.

I was very weary, for I had attended the closing exercises of the school that day; but I now arose from the bed where I was lying and read to him for three hours.

His heart was softened, tears were in his eyes, and when I ceased reading, he said, "I accept every word; all of it belongs to me." Much of the matter I had read related to the Echo office and its management from the beginning. The Lord also revealed to me Brother Faulkhead's connection with the Free Masons, and plainly stated that unless he severed every tie that bound him to these associations he would lose his soul.

He said, "I accept the light the Lord has sent me through you. I will act upon it. I am a member of five lodges, and three other lodges are under my control. I transact all of their business. Now I shall attend no more of their meetings, and shall close my business relations with them as fast as possible." I repeated to him the words spoken by my guide in reference to these associations. Giving a certain movement that was made by my guide, I said, "I cannot relate all that was given to me."

Brother Faulkhead told Elder Daniells and others that I gave the particular sign known only by the highest order of Masons, which he had just entered. He said that I did not know the sign, and that I was not aware that I was giving the sign to him. This was special evidence to him that the Lord was working through me to save his soul.—5MR 148, 149.

Angelic Presences While
Ellen White Was Awake

When I awoke and looked out of the window, I saw two white clouds. Then I fell asleep again; and in my dreams these words were spoken to me: "Look at these clouds. It was just such clouds as these that enshrouded the heavenly host who proclaimed to the shepherds the birth of the world's Redeemer." I awoke and looked out of the car window again, and there were the two large white clouds, as white as snow. They were distinct, separate clouds, but one would approach and touch the other, and for a moment they would blend together; then they would separate, and remain as distinct as before. They did not disappear, but continued in sight throughout the forenoon. At twelve o'clock we changed cars, and I did not see the clouds any more.

During the day I was deeply impressed with the thought that angels of God, enshrouded in these clouds, were going before us; that we might rejoice in their guardianship, and also in the assurance that we should see of the salvation of God in the meetings to be held in Brisbane. And now that the meetings are over, and we have seen the wonderful interest manifested by the people, I am more than ever sure that heavenly angels were enshrouded in these clouds—angels that were sent from the courts above to move upon the hearts of the people, and to restrain those distracting influences that sometimes find access to our campgrounds, by which minds are diverted from the consideration of the vital truths which are daily presented.

At this meeting, thousands have heard the gospel invitation, and have listened to truths that they never have heard before. During the whole meeting, there has not been any boisterous opposition, or loud contention from those whose hearts are opposed to the law of God. And throughout the city, we hear of no public opposition. This is an unusual experience; and we believe that the angels of God have been present to press back the powers of darkness.—RH March 21, 1899.

I was suffering with rheumatism in my left side and could get no rest because of the pain. I turned from side to side, trying to find ease from the suffering. There was a pain in my heart that portended no good for me. At last I fell asleep.

About half past nine I attempted to turn myself, and as I did so, I became aware that my body was entirely free from pain. As I turned from side to side, and moved my hands, I experienced an extraordinary freedom and lightness that I cannot describe. The room was filled with light, a most beautiful, soft, azure light, and I seemed to be in the arms of heavenly beings.

This peculiar light I have experienced in the past in times of special blessing, but this time it was more distinct, more impressive, and I felt such peace, peace so full and abundant no words can express it. I raised myself into a sitting posture, and I saw that I was surrounded by a bright cloud, white as snow, the edges of which were tinged with a deep pink. The softest, sweetest music was filling the air, and I recognized the music as the singing of the angels. Then a Voice spoke to me, saying: "Fear not; I am your Saviour. Holy angels are all about you."—9T 65, 66.

20.

Angels in the Final Crisis

Good and Evil Angels Will Appear

Satanic agencies in human form will take part in this last great conflict to oppose the building up of the kingdom of God. And heavenly angels in human guise will be on the field of action. The two opposing parties will continue to exist till the closing up of the last great chapter in this world's history.—RH Aug. 5, 1909.

Satan will use every opportunity to seduce men from their allegiance to God. He and his evil angels who fell with him will appear on the earth as men, seeking to deceive. God's angels also will appear as men, and will use every means in their power to defeat the purposes of the enemy. We have a part to act.—8MR 399.

Satan brings all his powers to the assault in the last, close conflict, and the endurance of the follower of Christ is taxed to the utmost. At times it seems that he must yield. But a word of prayer to the Lord Jesus goes like an arrow to the throne of God, and angels of God are sent to the field of battle. The tide is turned. —HP 297.

In the closing period of earth's history the Lord will work mightily in behalf of those who stand steadfastly for the right. . . . Angels that excel in strength will protect them.—PK 513.

The Work of Evil Angels Through Spiritualism

Satan has long been preparing for his final effort to deceive the world. . . . Little by little he has prepared the way for his masterpiece of deception in the development of Spiritualism. He has not yet reached the full accomplishment of his designs; but it will be reached in the last remnant of time. . . . Except those who are kept by the power of God, through faith in His Word, the whole world will be swept into the ranks of this delusion.—GC 561, 562.

Spiritualism is the masterpiece of deception. It is Satan's most successful and fascinating delusion—one calculated to take hold of the sympathies of those who have laid their loved ones in the grave. Evil angels come in the form of those loved ones, and relate incidents connected with their lives, and perform acts which they performed while living. In this way they lead persons to believe that their dead friends are angels, hovering over them and communicating with them. These evil angels, who assume to be the deceased friends, are regarded with a certain idolatry, and with many their word has greater weight than the Word of God.—ST Aug. 26, 1889.

The coming of the Lord is to be preceded by "the working of Satan with all power and signs and lying won-

ders, and with all deceivableness of unrighteousness."
And the apostle John, describing the miracle-working
power that will be manifested in the last days, declares:
"He doeth great wonders, so that he maketh fire come
down from heaven on the earth in the sight of men, and
deceiveth them that dwell on the earth by the means of
those miracles which he had power to do." No mere impostures are here foretold. Men are deceived by the
miracles which Satan's agents have power to do, not
which they pretend to do.—GC 553.

Satan is a cunning foe. And it is not difficult for the
evil angels to represent both saints and sinners who have
died, and make these representations visible to human
eyes. These manifestations will be more frequent, and
developments of a more startling character will appear
as we near the close of time.—RH April 1, 1875.

He [Satan] has power to bring before men the appearance of their departed friends. The counterfeit is
perfect; the familiar look, the words, the tone, are re-
produced with marvelous distinctness. . . .

Many will be confronted by the spirits of devils personating beloved relatives or friends, and declaring the
most dangerous heresies. These visitants will appeal
to our tenderest sympathies, and will work miracles to
sustain their pretensions. We must be prepared to withstand them with the Bible truth that the dead know
not anything, and that they who thus appear are the
spirits of devils.

Just before us is the "hour of temptation, which
shall come upon all the world, to try them that dwell

upon the earth." All whose faith is not firmly established upon the Word of God will be deceived and overcome.—GC 552, 560.

Communications from the spirits will declare that God has sent them to convince the rejecters of Sunday of their error, affirming that the laws of the land should be obeyed as the law of God. They will lament the great wickedness in the world, and second the testimony of religious teachers, that the degraded state of morals is caused by the desecration of Sunday. Great will be the indignation excited against all who refuse to accept their testimony.—GC 591.

Miracles in the End Time

Before the close of time he [Satan] will work still greater wonders. So far as his power extends, he will perform actual miracles. Says the Scripture: "He . . . deceiveth them that dwell on the earth by the means of those miracles which he had power to do," not merely those which he pretends to do. Something more than mere impostures is brought to view in this scripture. —5T 698.

We need not be deceived. Wonderful scenes, with which Satan will be closely connected, will soon take place. God's Word declares that Satan will work miracles. He will make people sick, and then will suddenly remove from them his satanic power. They will then be regarded as healed. These works of apparent healing will bring Seventh-day Adventists to the test.—2SM 53.

Some will be tempted to receive these wonders as from God. The sick will be healed before us. Miracles will be performed in our sight. Are we prepared for the trial which awaits us when the lying wonders of Satan shall be more fully exhibited? Will not many souls be ensnared and taken? By departing from the plain precepts and commandments of God, and giving heed to fables, the minds of many are preparing to receive these lying wonders. We must all now seek to arm ourselves for the contest in which we must soon engage. Faith in God's Word, prayerfully studied and practically applied, will be our shield from Satan's power and will bring us off conquerors through the blood of Christ.—1T 302.

Evil Spirits Active Among the Remnant

The forms of the dead will appear through the cunning device of Satan, and many will link up with the one who loveth and maketh a lie. . . . Right among us some will turn away from the faith and give heed to seducing spirits and doctrines of devils.—UL 317.

Spiritualists will press the matter to engage in controversy with ministers who teach the truth. If they decline, they will dare them. They quote Scripture, as did Satan to Christ. "Prove all things," they say. But their idea of proving is to listen to their deceptive reasonings, and attend their circles. But in their gatherings the angels of darkness assume the forms of dead friends, and communicate with them as angels of light.

Their loved ones will appear in robes of light, as

familiar to the sight as when they were upon the earth. They will teach them, and converse with them. And many will be deceived by this wonderful display of Satan's power. The only safety for the people of God is to be thoroughly conversant with their Bibles, and be intelligent upon the reasons of our faith in regard to the sleep of the dead.—ST April 12, 1883.

Evil angels in the form of believers will work in our ranks to bring in a strong spirit of unbelief. Let not even this discourage you, but bring a true heart to the help of the Lord against the powers of satanic agencies. These powers of evil will assemble in our meetings, not to receive a blessing, but to counterwork the influence of the Spirit of God. . . .

We are never to catch up the words that human lips may speak to confirm the evil angels in their work, but we should repeat the words of Christ. Christ was the Instructor in the assemblies of these angels before they fell from their high estate.—3SM 410.

Satan and his angels will appear on this earth as men, and will mingle with those of whom God's Word says, "Some shall depart from the faith, giving heed to seducing spirits, and doctrines of devils."—8MR 345.

When these spiritualistic deceptions are revealed to be what they really are—the secret workings of evil spirits—those who have acted a part in them will become as men who have lost their minds.—8MR 345.

I saw our people in great distress, weeping and praying, pleading the sure promises of God, while the wicked were all around us, mocking us, and threatening to destroy us. They ridiculed our feebleness, they mocked at the smallness of our numbers, and taunted us with words calculated to cut deep. They charged us with taking an independent position from all the rest of the world. They had cut off our resources so that we could not buy nor sell, and referred to our abject poverty and stricken condition. They could not see how we could live without the world; we were dependent upon the world, and we must concede to the customs, practices, and laws of the world, or go out of it. If we were the only people in the world whom the Lord favored, the appearances were awfully against us.

They declared that they had the truth, that miracles were among them, that angels from heaven talked with them and walked with them, that great power, and signs and wonders were performed among them, and this was the Temporal Millennium, which they had been expecting so long. The whole world was converted and in harmony with the Sunday law, and this little feeble people stood out in defiance of the laws of the land and the laws of God, and claimed to be the only ones right on the earth.—Mar 209.

Angels Will Do the Work Men Neglected

When divine power is combined with human effort, the work will spread like fire in the stubble. God will employ agencies whose origin man will not be able to discern; angels will do a work which men might have had the blessing of accomplishing, had they not neglected the claims of God.—RH Dec. 15, 1885.

Angels Will Supply the Needs of God's People

I saw the saints leaving the cities and villages, and associating together in companies, and living in the most solitary places. Angels provided them food and water, while the wicked were suffering from hunger and thirst.—EW 282.

In the time of trouble just before the coming of Christ, the righteous will be preserved through the ministration of heavenly angels; but there will be no security for the transgressor of God's law. Angels cannot then protect those who are disregarding one of the divine precepts.—PP 256.

In the midst of the time of trouble—trouble such as has not been since there was a nation—His chosen ones will stand unmoved. Satan with all the hosts of evil cannot destroy the weakest of God's saints. Angels that excel in strength will protect them, and in their behalf Jehovah will reveal Himself as a "God of gods," able to save to the uttermost those who have put their trust in Him.—PK 513.

Satan's Personations

In this age antichrist will appear as the true Christ, and then the law of God will be fully made void in the nations of our world. Rebellion against God's holy law will be fully ripe. But the true leader of all this rebellion is Satan clothed as an angel of light. Men will be deceived and will exalt him to the place of God, and deify him. But Omnipotence will interpose, and to the apostate churches that unite in the exaltation of Satan, the sentence will go forth, "Therefore shall her plagues come in one day, death, and mourning, and famine; and she shall be utterly burned with fire: for strong is the Lord God who judgeth her."—TM 62.

Disguised as an angel of light, he [Satan] will walk the earth as a wonder-worker. In beautiful language he will present lofty sentiments. Good words will be spoken by him, and good deeds performed. Christ will be personified, but on one point there will be a marked distinction. Satan will turn the people from the law of God. Notwithstanding this, so well will he counterfeit righteousness, that if it were possible, he would deceive the very elect. Crowned heads, presidents, rulers in high places, will bow to his false theories.—RH Aug. 17, 1897.

It is impossible to give any idea of the experience of the people of God who shall be alive upon the earth when celestial glory and a repetition of the persecutions of the past are blended. They will walk in the light proceeding from the throne of God. By means of the angels there will be constant communication between heaven and earth. And Satan, surrounded by evil angels, and claiming to be God, will work miracles of all kinds, to deceive, if possible, the very elect. God's people will not find their safety in working miracles, for Satan will counterfeit the miracles that will be wrought.—9T 16.

Satan is preparing his deceptions that in his last campaign against the people of God, they may not understand that it is he. "And no marvel; for Satan himself is transformed into an angel of light." . . . Satan will go to the extent of his power to harass, tempt, and mislead God's people.—RH May 13, 1862.

Satan . . . will come personating Jesus Christ, working mighty miracles; and men will fall down and worship him as Jesus Christ. We shall be commanded to worship this being, whom the world will glorify as Christ. What shall we do?—Tell them that Christ has warned us against just such a foe, who is man's worst enemy, yet who claims to be God.—RH Dec. 18, 1888.

The time is coming when Satan will work miracles right in your sight, claiming that he is Christ; and if your feet are not firmly established upon the truth of God, then you will be led away from your foundation. —RH April 3, 1888.

In the last days he [Satan] will appear in such a manner as to make men believe him to be Christ come the second time into the world. He will indeed transform himself into an angel of light. But while he will bear the appearance of Christ in every particular, so far as mere appearance goes, it will deceive none but those who . . . are seeking to resist the truth.—5T 698.

Evil Angels Incite Persecution

Satan is at work from beneath to stir up the hellish

powers of his confederacy of evil against the just. He imbues human agencies with his own attributes. Evil angels united with evil men will put forth efforts to harass, persecute, and destroy.—UL 262.

With every rejection of truth, the minds of the people will become darker, their hearts more stubborn, until they are entrenched in an infidel hardihood. In defiance of the warnings which God has given, they will continue to trample upon one of the precepts of the decalogue, until they are led to persecute those who hold it sacred. Christ is set at naught in the contempt placed upon His Word and His people. As the teachings of Spiritualism are accepted by the churches, the restraint imposed upon the carnal heart is removed, and the profession of religion will become a cloak to conceal the basest iniquity. A belief in spiritual manifestations opens the door to seducing spirits, and doctrines of devils, and thus the influence of evil angels will be felt in the churches.—GC 603, 604.

The scenes of the betrayal, rejection, and crucifixion of Christ have been reenacted, and will again be reenacted on an immense scale. People will be filled with the attributes of Satan. The delusions of the archenemy of God and man will have great power.—3SM 415.

A demoniacal spirit takes possession of men in our world. . . . Demon intelligence . . . will rend and destroy man formed in the divine similitude because . . . [man] cannot control the conscience of his brother and make him disloyal to God's holy law.—UL 285.

As the saints left the cities and villages, they were pursued by the wicked, who sought to slay them. But the swords that were raised to kill God's people broke and fell as powerless as a straw. Angels of God shielded the saints.—EW 284, 285.

In the day of fierce trial He [Christ] will say, "Come, My people, enter thou into thy chambers, and shut thy doors about thee: hide thyself as it were for a little moment, until the indignation be overpast." What are the chambers in which they are to hide? They are the protection of Christ and holy angels. The people of God are not at this time all in one place. They are in different companies, and in all parts of the world.—HS 158.

In the closing scenes of this earth's history, when intensity is taking possession of every earthly element, the Lord requires of us a vigilance that knows no relaxation. But we are not left to struggle alone. Amid the dangers increasing on every hand, those who walk humbly before God, distrustful of their own wisdom, will have angels as their helpers and protectors. In times of special peril they will know the power of God's keeping care.—RH April 25, 1907.

During the night a very impressive scene passed before me. There seemed to be great confusion and the conflict of armies. A messenger from the Lord stood before me, and said, "Call your household. I will lead you; follow me." He led me down a dark passage, through a forest, then through the clefts of mountains, and said, "Here you are safe." There were others who had been led to this retreat. The heavenly messenger said, "The time of trouble has come as a thief in the night, as the Lord warned you it would come."—Mar 270.

Satan's Personation After the Close of Probation

The wrath of Satan increases as his time grows short, and his work of deceit and destruction reaches its culmination in the time of trouble. God's long-suffering has ended. The world has rejected His mercy, despised His love, and trampled upon His law. The wicked have passed the boundary of their probation, and the Lord withdraws His protection, and leaves them to the mercy of the leader they have chosen. . . .

As the crowning act in the great drama of deception, Satan himself will attempt to personate Christ. The church has long professed to look to the Saviour's advent as the consummation of her hopes. Now the great deceiver will make it appear that Christ has come. In different parts of the earth, Satan will manifest himself among men as a majestic being of dazzling brightness, resembling the description of the Son of God given by John in the Revelation. The glory that surrounds him is unsurpassed by anything that mortal eyes have yet beheld. The shout of triumph rings out upon the air, "Christ has come! Christ has come!"

The people prostrate themselves in adoration before him, while he lifts up his hands, and pronounces a blessing upon them, as Christ blessed His disciples when He was personally upon the earth. His voice is soft and subdued, yet full of melody. In gentle, compassionate tones he presents some of the same gracious, heavenly truths which the Saviour uttered; he heals the diseases of the people, and then, in his assumed character of Christ, he claims to have changed the Sabbath to Sunday, and commands all to hallow the day which he has blessed. He declares that those who persist in keeping holy the seventh day are blaspheming his name by refusing to listen to his angels sent to them with light and truth. This is the strong, almost overmastering delusion.—4SP 441, 442.

Satan sees that he is about to lose his case. He cannot sweep in the whole world. He makes one last desperate effort to overcome the faithful by deception. He does this in personating Christ. He clothes himself with the garments of royalty which have been accurately described in the vision of John. He has power to do this. He will appear to his deluded followers, the Christian world who received not the love of the truth but had pleasure in unrighteousness . . . as Christ coming the second time.

He proclaims himself Christ, and he is believed to be Christ, a beautiful, majestic being clothed with majesty and, with soft voice and pleasant words, with glory unsurpassed by anything their mortal eyes had yet beheld. Then his deceived, deluded followers set up a shout of victory, "Christ has come the second time! Christ has come! He has lifted up His hands just as He did when He was upon the earth, and blessed us." . . .

The saints look on with amazement. Will they also be deceived? Will they worship Satan? Angels of God are about them. A clear, firm, musical voice is heard, "Look up."

There is one object before the praying ones—the final and eternal salvation of their souls. This object was before them constantly—that immortal life was promised to those who endure unto the end. Oh, how earnest and fervent had been their desires. The judgment and eternity were in view. Their eyes by faith were fixed on the blazing throne, before which the white-robed ones were to stand. This restrained them from the indulgence of sin. . . .

One effort more, and then Satan's last device is employed. He hears the unceasing cry for Christ to come, for Christ to deliver them. This last strategy is to personate Christ, and make them think their prayers are answered.—LDE 164, 165.

Angels and the Universal Death Decree

Could men see with heavenly vision, they would behold companies of angels that excel in strength stationed about those who have kept the word of Christ's patience. With sympathizing tenderness, angels have witnessed their distress, and have heard their prayers. They are waiting the word of their Commander to snatch them from their peril. But they must wait a little longer. The people of God must drink of the cup, and be baptized with the baptism. The very delay, so painful to them, is the best answer to their petitions. As they endeavor to wait trustingly for the Lord to work, they are led to exercise faith, hope, and patience, which have been too little exercised during their religious experience. . . .

The heavenly sentinels, faithful to their trust, continue their watch. Though a general decree has fixed the time when commandment-keepers may be put to death, their enemies will in some cases anticipate the decree, and before the time specified, will endeavor to take their lives. But none can pass the mighty guardians stationed about every faithful soul.—GC 630, 631.

God Interposes as the Wicked Try to Kill God's People

The people of God—some in prison cells, some hidden in solitary retreats in the forests and the mountains—still plead for divine protection, while in every quarter companies of armed men, urged on by hosts of evil angels, are preparing for the work of death. It is now, in the hour of utmost extremity, that the God of Israel will interpose for the deliverance of His chosen. . . .

It is at midnight that God manifests His power for the deliverance of His people. The sun appears, shining in its strength. Signs and wonders follow in quick succession. The wicked look with terror and amazement upon the scene, while the righteous behold with solemn joy the tokens of their deliverance. . . . Dark, heavy clouds come up, and clash against each other. In the midst of the angry heavens is one clear space of indescribable glory, whence comes the voice of God. . . .

That voice shakes the heavens and the earth. There is a mighty earthquake, "such as was not since men were upon the earth, so mighty an earthquake, and so great." The firmament appears to open and shut. The glory from the throne of God seems flashing through. The mountains shake like a reed in the wind, and ragged rocks are scattered on every side. There is a roar as of a coming tempest. The sea is lashed into fury. There is heard the shriek of the hurricane, like the voice of demons upon a mission of destruction. The whole earth heaves and swells like the waves of the sea. Its surface is breaking up. Its very foundations seem to be giving way. Mountain chains are sinking. Inhabited islands disappear. . . .

Fierce lightnings leap from the heavens, enveloping the earth in a sheet of flames. Above the terrific roar of thunder, voices, mysterious and awful, declare the doom of the wicked. . . . Those who a little before were so reckless, so boastful and defiant, so exultant in their cruelty to God's commandment-keeping people, are now overwhelmed with consternation, and shuddering in fear. Their wails are heard above the sound of the elements. Demons acknowledge the deity of Christ, and tremble before His power, while men are supplicating for mercy, and groveling in abject terror. —GC 635-638.

The Second Coming of Christ

Christ is coming with power and great glory. He is coming with His own glory, and with the glory of the Father. He is coming with all the holy angels with Him. While all the world is plunged in darkness, there will be light in every dwelling of the saints. They will catch the first light of His second appearing.—COL 420.

Soon our eyes were drawn to the east, for a small black cloud had appeared, about half as large as a man's hand, which we all knew was the sign of the Son of man. In solemn silence we all gazed on the cloud as it drew nearer, and became lighter, glorious, and still more glorious, till it was a great white cloud. The bottom appeared like fire; a rainbow was over the cloud, while around it were ten thousand angels, singing a most lovely song; and upon it sat the Son of Man.—1T 60.

No human language can portray the scenes of the second coming of the Son of man in the clouds of heaven. . . . He will come clad in the robe of light, which He has worn from the days of eternity.—RH Sept. 5, 1899.

A holy retinue of angels, with their bright, glittering crowns upon their heads, escorted Him on His way.—1SG 206, 207.

Amid the reeling of the earth, the flash of lightning, and the roar of thunder, the voice of the Son of God calls forth the sleeping saints. He looks upon the graves of the righteous, then, raising His hands to heaven, He cries, "Awake, awake, awake, ye that sleep in the dust, and arise!" . . .

All come forth from their graves the same in stature as when they entered the tomb. Adam, who stands among the risen throng, is of lofty height and majestic form, in stature but little below the Son of God. He presents a marked contrast to the people of later generations; in this one respect is shown the great degeneracy of the race. But all arise with the freshness and vigor of eternal youth. . . . The mortal, corruptible form, devoid of comeliness, once polluted with sin, becomes perfect, beautiful, and immortal. All blemishes and deformities are left in the grave.—GC 644, 645.

He [Christ] died for us, and was raised for us, that we might come forth from the tomb to a glorious companionship with heavenly angels, to meet our loved ones and to recognize their faces, for the Christlikeness does not destroy their image, but transforms it into His glorious image. Every saint connected in family relationship here will know each other there.—3SM 316.

The living righteous are changed "in a moment, in the twinkling of an eye." At the voice of God they were glorified: now they are made immortal, and with the risen saints are caught up to meet their Lord in the air. Angels "gather together the elect from the four winds, from one end of heaven to the other."—GC 645.

Little children are borne by holy angels to their mothers' arms.—GC 645.

As the little infants come forth immortal from their dusty beds, they immediately wing their way to their mother's arms. They meet again nevermore to part. But many of the little ones have no mother there. We listen in vain for the rapturous song of triumph from the mother. The angels receive the motherless infants and conduct them to the tree of life.—YI April 1, 1858.

Friends long separated by death are united, nevermore to part, and with songs of gladness ascend together to the city of God.

On each side of the cloudy chariot are wings, and beneath it are living wheels; and as the chariot rolls upward, the wheels cry, "Holy," and the wings, as they move, cry, "Holy," and the retinue of angels cry, "Holy, holy, holy, Lord God Almighty." And the redeemed shout, "Alleluia!" as the chariot moves onward toward the New Jerusalem.—GC 645.

We all entered the cloud together, and were seven days ascending to the sea of glass, when Jesus brought the crowns, and with His own right hand placed them on our heads. He gave us harps of gold and palms of victory.—EW 16.

There are the columns of angels on either side, and the ransomed of God walk in through the cherubims and seraphims. Christ bids them welcome and puts upon them His benediction. "Well done, thou good and faithful servant: . . . enter thou into the joy of thy Lord."—6BC 1093.

Satan and His Evil Angels Confined to This Earth

The whole earth appears like a desolate wilderness. The ruins of cities and villages destroyed by the earthquake, uprooted trees, ragged rocks thrown out by the sea or torn out of the earth itself, are scattered over its surface, while vast caverns mark the spot where the mountains have been rent from their foundations. Here is to be the home of Satan with his evil angels for a thousand years. Here he will be confined, to wander up and down over the broken surface of the earth, and see the effects of his rebellion against the law of God. For a thousand years he can enjoy the fruit of the curse which he has caused. Limited alone to the earth, he will not have the privilege of ranging to other planets, to tempt and annoy those who have not fallen.—4SP 474, 475.

By his own course of action Satan has forged a chain by which he will be bound. . . . All the unfallen beings are now united in regarding God's law as changeless. They support the government of Him, who, to redeem the transgressor, spared not His own Son. His law has been proved faultless. His government is forever secure.—ST Aug. 27, 1902.

Here is to be the home of Satan with his evil angels for a thousand years. Limited to the earth, he will not have access to other worlds to tempt and annoy those who have never fallen. It is in this sense that he is bound.—GC 659.

I heard shouts of triumph from the angels and from the redeemed saints, which sounded like ten thousand musical instruments, because they were to be no more annoyed and tempted by Satan, and because the inhabitants of other worlds were delivered from his presence and his temptations.—EW 290.

21.

Angels in the Great Hereafter

When We Get to Heaven

I saw a very great number of angels bring from the city glorious crowns—a crown for every saint, with his name written thereon. As Jesus called for the crowns, angels presented them to Him, and with His own right hand the lovely Jesus placed the crowns on the heads of the saints. In the same manner the angels brought the harps, and Jesus presented them also to the saints. The commanding angels first struck the note, and then every voice was raised in grateful, happy praise, and every hand skillfully swept over the strings of the harp, sending forth melodious music in rich and perfect strains. Then I saw Jesus lead the redeemed company to the gate of the city. He laid hold of the gate and swung it back on its glittering hinges, and bade the nations that had kept the truth enter in.—EW 288.

From the lips of the King of glory the benediction will fall upon their ears like richest music, "Come, ye blessed of my Father, inherit the kingdom prepared for you from the foundation of the world." Thus the redeemed will be welcomed to the mansions that Jesus is preparing for them. There their companions will not be the vile of earth, but those who through divine aid have formed perfect characters. Every sinful tendency, every imperfection, has been removed by the blood of Christ; and the excellence and brightness of His glory, far exceeding the brightness of the sun in its meridian splendor, is imparted to them. And the moral beauty, the perfection of His character, shines through them, in worth far exceeding this outward splendor. They are without fault before the great white throne, sharing the dignity and privileges of the angels.—*The Watchman,* March 31, 1908.

The redeemed will meet and recognize those whose attention they have directed to the uplifted Saviour. What blessed converse they have with these souls! "I was a sinner," it will be said, "without God and without hope in the world, and you came to me and drew my attention to the precious Saviour as my only hope. . . ." Others will say, "I was a heathen in heathen lands. You left your friends and comfortable home and came to teach me how to find Jesus, and believe in Him as the only true God. I demolished my idols, and worshiped God, and now I see Him face to face. I am saved, eternally saved, ever to behold Him whom I love. . . ."

Others will express their gratitude to those who fed the hungry and clothed the naked. "When despair bound my soul in unbelief, the Lord sent you to me," they say, "to speak words of hope and comfort. You brought me food for my physical necessities, and you opened to me the Word of God, awakening me to my spiritual needs. You treated me as a brother. You sympathized with me in my sorrows, and restored my bruised and wounded soul, so that I could grasp the hand of Christ that was reached out to save me. In my ignorance you taught me patiently that I had a Father in heaven who cared for me. You read to me the precious promises of God's Word. You inspired in me the faith that He would save me. My heart was softened, subdued, broken, as I contemplated the sacrifice which Christ had made for me. . . . I am here, saved, eternally saved, ever to live in His presence, and to praise Him who gave His life for me."

What rejoicing there will be as these redeemed ones meet and greet those who have had a burden in their behalf!—RH Jan. 5, 1905.

If they [the youth] receive Christ and believe in Him, they will be brought into close relationship with God. He gives them power to become the sons of God, to associate with the highest dignitaries in the kingdom of heaven, to unite with Gabriel, with cherubim and seraphim, with angels and the archangel. "And he showed me a pure river of water of life, clear as crystal, proceeding out of the throne of God and of the Lamb. In the midst of the street of it, and on either side of the river, was there the tree of life, which bare twelve manner of fruits, and yielded her fruit every month; and the leaves of the tree were for the healing of the nations. And there shall be no more curse; but the throne of God and of the Lamb shall be in it; and His servants shall serve Him. And they shall see His face, and His name shall be in their foreheads. And there shall be no night there; and they need no candle, neither light of the sun; for the

Lord God giveth them light; and they shall reign forever and ever."—*Spaulding and Magan Collection* 52.

Not until the providences of God are seen in the light of eternity shall we understand what we owe to the care and interposition of His angels. Celestial beings have taken an active part in the affairs of men.—Ed 304.

In the future life we shall understand things that here greatly perplex us. We shall realize how strong a helper we had, and how angels of God were commissioned to guard us as we followed the counsel of the Word of God.—ST Jan. 3, 1906.

In the world to come, Christ will lead the redeemed beside the river of life, and will teach them wonderful lessons of truth. He will unfold to them the mysteries of nature. They will see that a Master-Hand holds the worlds in position. They will behold the skill displayed by the great Artist in coloring the flowers of the field, and will learn of the purposes of the merciful Father, who dispenses every ray of light, and with the holy angels the redeemed will acknowledge in songs of grateful praise God's supreme love to an unthankful world. Then it will be understood that "God so loved the world, that he gave his only begotten Son, that whosoever believeth in him should not perish, but have everlasting life."—RH Jan. 3, 1907.

They [the heirs of grace] have even a more sacred relationship to God than have the angels who have never fallen.—5T 740.

By the power of His love, through obedience, fallen man, a worm of the dust, is to be transformed, fitted to be a member of the heavenly family, a companion through eternal ages of God and Christ and the holy angels. Heaven will triumph, for the vacancies made by the fall of Satan and his host will be filled by the redeemed of the Lord.—UL 61.

God created man for His own glory, that after test and trial the human family might become one with the heavenly family. It was God's purpose to repopulate heaven with the human family, if they would show themselves obedient to His every word. Adam was to be tested, to see whether he would be obedient, as the loyal angels, or disobedient.—1BC 1082.

The loves and sympathies which God Himself has planted in the soul, shall there find truest and sweetest exercise. The pure communion with holy beings, the harmonious social life with the blessed angels and with the faithful ones of all ages who have washed their robes and made them white in the blood of the Lamb, the sacred ties that bind together "the whole family in heaven and earth" (Ephesians 3:15)—these help to constitute the happiness of the redeemed.—GC 677.

The Millennial Judgment

During the thousand years between the first and the second resurrection, the judgment of the wicked takes place. Daniel declares that when the Ancient of days came, "judgment was given to the saints of the Most High." At this time the righteous reign as kings and priests unto God. John in the Revelation says, "I saw thrones, and they sat upon them, and judgment was given unto them." "They shall be priests of God and of Christ, and shall reign with him a thousand years." It is at this time that, as foretold by Paul, "the saints shall judge the world." In union with Christ they judge the wicked, comparing their acts with the statute book, the Bible, and deciding every case according to the deeds done in the body. Satan also and evil angels are judged by Christ and His people.—SW, March 14, 1905.

The Third Coming of Christ

At the close of the thousand years, Christ again returns to the earth. He is accompanied by the host of the redeemed, and attended by a retinue of angels. As He descends in terrific majesty, He bids the wicked dead arise to receive their doom. They come forth, a mighty host, numberless as the sands of the sea. What a contrast to those who were raised at the first resurrection! The righteous were clothed with immortal youth and beauty. The wicked bear the traces of disease and death.

Every eye in that vast multitude is turned to behold the glory of the Son of God. With one voice the wicked hosts exclaim, "Blessed is He that cometh in the name of the Lord!" It is not love to Jesus that inspires this utterance. The force of truth urges the words from unwilling lips. As the wicked went into their graves, so they come forth, with the same enmity to

Christ, and the same spirit of rebellion. They are to have no new probation, in which to remedy the defects of their past lives. Nothing would be gained by this. A lifetime of transgression has not softened their hearts. A second probation, were it given them, would be occupied as was the first, in evading the requirements of God and exciting rebellion against Him.

Christ descends upon the Mount of Olives, whence, after His resurrection, He ascended, and where angels repeated the promise of His return. Says the prophet: "The Lord my God shall come, and all the saints with Thee." "And His feet shall stand in that day upon the Mount of Olives, which is before Jerusalem on the east, and the Mount of Olives shall cleave in the midst thereof, . . . and there shall be a very great valley." "And the Lord shall be king over all the earth: in that day shall there be one Lord, and His name one." Zechariah 14:5, 4, 9.—GC 662, 663.

Then we looked up and saw the great and beautiful City, with twelve foundations, twelve gates, three on each side, and an angel at each gate. We cried out, The City! The great City! It is coming down from God out of heaven! And it came down in all its splendor, and dazzling glory, and settled in the mighty plain which Jesus had prepared for it.—1SG 213.

Now Satan prepares for a last mighty struggle for the supremacy. While deprived of his power, and cut off from his work of deception, the prince of evil was miserable and dejected; but as the wicked dead are raised, and he sees the vast multitudes upon his side, his hopes revive, and he determines not to yield the great controversy. . . . The wicked are Satan's captives. . . . They are ready to receive his suggestions and to do his bidding. Yet, true to his early cunning, he does not acknowledge himself to be Satan. He claims to be the prince who is the rightful owner of the world, and whose inheritance has been unlawfully wrested from him. He represents himself to his deluded subjects as a redeemer, assuring them that his power has brought them forth from their graves, and that he is about to rescue them from the most cruel tyranny. . . . He proposes to lead them against the camp of the saints, and to take possession of the city of God. . . .

In that vast throng are multitudes of the long-lived race that existed before the Flood. . . . There are kings and generals who conquered nations, valiant men who never lost a battle. . . . Satan consults with his angels, and then with these kings and conquerors and mighty men. They look upon the strength and numbers on their side, and declare that the army within the city is small in comparison with theirs, and that it can be overcome. They lay their plans to take possession of the riches and glory of the New Jerusalem. All immediately begin to prepare for battle. Skillful artisans construct implements of war. Military leaders, famed for their success, marshal the throngs of warlike men into companies and divisions.

At last the order to advance is given, and the countless host moves on. . . . Satan, the mightiest of warriors, leads the van, and his angels unite their forces for this final struggle.—GC 663, 664.

Now Christ again appears to the view of His enemies. Far above the city, upon a foundation of burnished gold, is a throne, high and lifted up. Upon this throne sits the Son of God, and around Him are the subjects of His kingdom.—GC 665.

In the presence of the assembled inhabitants of earth and heaven the final coronation of the Son of God takes place. . . .

He [Satan] has seen the crown placed upon the head of Christ by an angel of lofty stature and majestic presence, and he knows that the exalted position of this angel might have been his.—GC 666, 669.

The Last Judgment

Now, invested with supreme majesty and power, the King of kings pronounces sentence upon the rebels against His government, and executes justice upon those who have transgressed His law and oppressed His people. . . .

As soon as the books of record are opened, and the eye of Jesus looks upon the wicked, they are conscious of every sin which they have ever committed. They see just where their feet diverged from the path of purity and holiness, just how far pride and rebellion have carried them in the violation of the law of God. . . .

Above the throne is revealed the cross; and like a panoramic view appear the scenes of Adam's temptation and fall, and the successive steps in the great plan of redemption. The Saviour's lowly birth; His early life of simplicity and obedience; His baptism in Jordan; . . .

His public ministry; . . . His betrayal . . . ; the Son of God exultingly displayed before Annas, arraigned in the high priest's palace, in the judgment hall of Pilate, before the cowardly and cruel Herod . . .—all are vividly portrayed.

And now before the swaying multitude are revealed the final scenes—the patient Sufferer treading the path to Calvary; the Prince of heaven hanging upon the cross. . . .

The awful spectacle appears just as it was. Satan, his angels, and his subjects have no power to turn from the picture of their own work. Each actor recalls the part which he performed.—GC 666, 667.

The time will come when all must stand before angels and before men, revealed in their true light. As the artist reproduces upon the polished plate the features of the human countenance, so their characters are being transferred to the books of heaven. . . . In the judgment every man will stand revealed just as he is, either fashioned after the divine similitude or disfigured by the idolatrous sins of selfishness and covetousness. —17MR 288.

In the day when everyone shall be rewarded according as his work has been, how will transgressors appear in their own sight as for a few moments they are permitted to see the record of their life as they have chosen to make it. . . .

In the day of judgment men will see what they might have become through the power of Christ. . . . They knew the claims of God, but they refused to comply with the conditions laid down in His Word. By their own choice they were united with demons. . . .

In the day of judgment, all this opens up before the impenitent. Scene after scene passes before them. As plainly as in the light of the noonday sun, they all see what they might have been had they cooperated with God instead of opposing Him. The picture cannot be changed. Their cases are forever decided. . . .

And the fallen angels, endowed with higher intelligence than man, will realize what they have done in using their powers to lead human beings to choose deception and falsehood.—UL 203.

But the time has now come when the rebellion is to be finally defeated and the history and character of Satan disclosed. In his last great effort to dethrone Christ, destroy His people, and take possession of the city of God, the archdeceiver has been fully unmasked. Those who have united with him see the total failure of his cause. Christ's followers and the loyal angels behold the full extent of his machinations against the government of God. He is the object of universal abhorrence.

Satan sees that his voluntary rebellion has unfitted him for heaven. . . . His accusations against the mercy and justice of God are now silenced. The reproach which he has endeavored to cast upon Jehovah rests wholly upon himself. And now Satan bows down, and confesses the justice of his sentence. . . . Every question of truth and error in the longstanding controversy has now been made plain. . . .

Notwithstanding that Satan has been constrained to acknowledge God's justice, and to bow to the supremacy of Christ, his character remains unchanged. The spirit of rebellion, like a mighty torrent, again bursts forth. Filled with frenzy, he determines not to yield the great controversy. The time has come for a last desperate struggle against the King of heaven. He rushes into the midst of his subjects, and endeavors to inspire them with his own fury, and arouse them to instant battle. But of all the countless millions whom he has allured into rebellion, there are none now to acknowledge his supremacy. His power is at an end. . . . Their rage is kindled against Satan and those who have been his agents in deception, and with the fury of demons they turn upon them. . . .

Fire comes down from God out of heaven. The earth is broken up. . . . Devouring flames burst from every yawning chasm. . . . The day has come that shall burn as an oven. The elements melt with fervent heat, the earth also, and the works that are therein are burned up. Malachi 4:1; 2 Peter 3:10. The earth's surface seems one molten mass—a vast, seething lake of fire. . . .

The wicked receive their recompense. . . . Some are destroyed as in a moment, while others suffer many days. All are punished "according to their deeds." The sins of the righteous having been transferred to Satan, he is made to suffer not only for his own rebellion, but for all the sins which he has caused God's people to commit. His punishment is to be far greater than that of those whom he has deceived. After all have perished who fell by his deceptions, he is still to live and suffer on. In the cleansing flames the wicked are at last destroyed.—GC 670-673.

By a life of rebellion, Satan and all who unite with him place themselves so out of harmony with God that His very presence is to them a consuming fire. The glory of Him who is love will destroy them.—DA 764.

The whole universe will have become witnesses to the nature and result of sin. And its utter extermination, which in the beginning would have brought fear to angels and dishonor to God, will now vindicate His love and establish His honor before the universe of beings who delight to do His will, and in whose heart is His law.—GC 504.

The fire that consumes the wicked purifies the earth. Every trace of the curse is swept away. No eternally burning hell will keep before the ransomed the fearful consequences of sin.

One reminder alone remains: our Redeemer will ever bear the marks of His crucifixion. Upon His wounded head, upon His side, His hands and feet, are the only traces of the cruel work that sin has wrought. —GC 674.

Sin is a mysterious, unexplainable thing. There was no reason for its existence; to seek to explain it is to seek to give a reason for it, and that would be to justify it. Sin appeared in a perfect universe, a thing that was shown to be inexcusable and exceeding sinful. The reason of its inception or development was never explained and never can be, even at the last great day when the judgment shall sit and the books be opened. . . . At that day it will be evident to all that there is not, and never was, any cause for sin. At the final condemnation of Satan and his angels and of all men who have finally identified themselves with him as transgressors of God's law, every mouth will be stopped. When the hosts of rebellion, from the first great rebel to the last transgressor, are asked why they have broken the law of God, they will be speechless. There will be no answer to give, no reason to assign that will carry the least weight.—ST April 28, 1890.

The inhabitants of all worlds will be convinced of the justice of the law in the overthrow of rebellion and the eradication of sin. . . . The working out of the plan of salvation reveals not only to men but to angels, the character of God, and through the ages of eternity the malignant character of sin will be understood by the cost to the Father and the Son of the redemption of a rebel race. In Christ, the Lamb slain from the foundation of the world, all worlds will behold the marks of the curse, and angels as well as men will ascribe honor and glory to the Redeemer through whom they are all made secure from apostasy.

The efficiency of the cross guards the redeemed race from the danger of a second fall. The life and death of Christ effectually unveils the deceptions of Satan, and refutes his claims. The sacrifice of Christ for a fallen world draws not only men, but angels unto Him [in] bonds of indissoluble union. Through the plan of salvation the justice and mercy of God are fully vindicated, and to all eternity rebellion will never again arise, affliction never again touch the universe of God.—*The Messenger*, June 7, 1893.

The Earth Made New

When God finally purifies the earth, it will appear like a boundless lake of fire. As God preserved the ark amid the commotions of the Flood, because it contained eight righteous persons, He will preserve the New Jerusalem, containing the faithful of all ages. . . . Although the whole earth, with the exception of that portion where the city rests, will be wrapped in a sea of liquid fire, yet the city is preserved as was the ark, by a miracle of Almighty power. It stands unharmed amid the devouring elements.—3SG 87.

The New Earth and Our Eternal Inheritance

He [Moses] saw the earth purified by fire and cleansed from every vestige of sin, every mark of the curse, and renovated and given to the saints to possess forever and ever.—10MR 158.

The plan of redemption will not be fully understood, even when the ransomed see as they are seen and know as they are known; but through the eternal ages new truth will continually unfold to the wondering and delighted mind.—GC 651.

In the plan of redemption there are heights and depths that eternity itself can never exhaust, marvels into which the angels desire to look. The redeemed only, of all created beings, have in their own experience known the actual conflict with sin; they have wrought with Christ, and, as even the angels could not do, have entered into the fellowship of His sufferings; will they have no testimony as to the science of redemption—nothing that will be of worth to unfallen beings?—Ed 308.

There are mysteries in the plan of redemption . . . that are to the heavenly angels subjects of continual amazement. The apostle Peter, speaking of the revelations given to the prophets of "the sufferings of Christ, and the glory that should follow," says that these are things which "the angels desire to look into."—5T 702.

The redeemed throng will range from world to world, and much of their time will be employed in searching out the mysteries of redemption. And throughout the whole stretch of eternity, this subject will be continually opening to their minds.—RH March 9, 1886.

The science of redemption is the science of all sciences; the science that is the study of the angels and of all the intelligences of the unfallen worlds; the science that engages the attention of our Lord and Saviour; the science that enters into the purpose brooded in the mind of the Infinite. . . ; the science that will be the study of God's redeemed throughout endless ages.—Ed 126.

God's wonderful purpose of grace, the mystery of redeeming love, is the theme into which "angels desire to look," and it will be their study throughout endless ages. Both the redeemed and the unfallen beings will find in the cross of Christ their science and their song. It will be seen that the glory shining in the face of Jesus is the glory of self-sacrificing love. In the light from Calvary it will be seen that the law of self-renouncing love is the law of life for earth and heaven; that the love which "seeketh not her own" has its source in the heart of God; and that in the meek and lowly One is manifested the character of Him who dwelleth in the light which no man can approach unto.—DA 19, 20.

And the years of eternity, as they roll, will bring richer and still more glorious revelations of God and of Christ. As knowledge is progressive, so will love, reverence, and happiness increase. The more men learn of God, the greater will be their admiration of His character. As Jesus opens before them the riches of redemption, and the amazing achievements in the great controversy with Satan, the hearts of the ransomed thrill with more fervent devotion, and with more rapturous joy they sweep the harps of gold; and ten thousand times ten thousand and thousands of thousands of voices unite to swell the mighty chorus of praise.

"And every creature which is in heaven, and on the earth, and under the earth, and such as are in the sea, and all that are in them, heard I saying, Blessing, and honor, and glory, and power, be unto Him that sitteth upon the throne, and unto the Lamb forever and ever." Revelation 5:13.

The great controversy is ended. Sin and sinners are no more. The entire universe is clean. One pulse of harmony and gladness beats through the vast creation. From Him who created all, flow life and light and gladness, throughout the realms of illimitable space. From the minutest atom to the greatest world, all things, animate and inanimate, in their unshadowed beauty and perfect joy, declare that God is love.—GC 678.

Epilogue

The theme of redemption is one that angels desire to look into; it will be the science and the song of the ransomed throughout the ceaseless ages of eternity. Is it not worthy of careful thought and study now?—*BE* Jan. 1, 1888.

As he [a Bible student] studies and meditates upon the themes into which "the angels desire to look" (1 Peter 1:12), he may have their companionship. He may follow the steps of the heavenly Teacher, and listen to His words as when He taught on the mountain and plain and sea. He may dwell in this world in the atmosphere of heaven, imparting to earth's sorrowing and tempted ones thoughts of hope and longings for holiness; himself coming closer and still closer into fellowship with the Unseen; like him of old who walked with God, drawing nearer and nearer the threshold of the eternal world, until the portals shall open and he shall enter there. He will find himself no stranger. The voices that will greet him are the voices of the holy ones, who, unseen, were on earth his companions—voices that here he learned to distinguish and love. He who through the Word of God has lived in fellowship with heaven, will find himself at home in heaven's companionship.—Ed 127.

The Lord would have our perceptions keen to understand that these mighty ones who visit our world have borne an active part in all the work which we have called our own. These heavenly beings are ministering angels, and they frequently disguise themselves in the form of human beings. As strangers they converse with those who are engaged in the work of God. In lonely places they have been the companions of the traveler in peril. In tempest-tossed ships angels in human form have spoken words of encouragement to allay fear and inspire hope in the hour of danger, and the passengers have thought that it was one of their number to whom they had never before spoken.—UL 84.

Let us keep the heart full of God's precious promises, that we may speak words that will be a comfort and strength to others. Thus we may learn the language of the heavenly angels, who, if we are faithful, will be our companions through the eternal ages.—YI Jan. 10, 1901.

In the future life we shall understand things that here greatly perplex us. We shall realize how strong a helper we had and how angels of God were commissioned to guard us as we followed the counsel of the Word of God.—HP 257.

Every redeemed one will understand the ministry of angels in his own life. The angel who was his guardian from his earliest moment; the angel who watched his steps, and covered his head in the day of peril; the angel who was with him in the valley of the shadow of death, who marked his resting place, who was the first to greet him in the resurrection morning—what will it be to hold converse with him, and to learn the history of divine interposition in the individual life, of heavenly cooperation in every work for humanity!—Ed 305.

Scripture Index

Subject Index

Abraham
by his faithfulness in
offering Isaac, gave
angels insight into the
plan of redemption 80
talked with angels as
with a friend 73

Adam
talked with angels
daily 49

Adam and Eve
driven from Eden by
angels 62
instructed by angels in
their garden work 49
joined in singing with
angels 52
pled to be allowed to
die instead of God's
Son 60
warned by angels
regarding Satan 51

Angels
are superior in nature
to humans 9
depend upon the Source
of life for their exist-
ence 26
existed before humans
9

have access to God's
presence at all times
14

Animals
collected by angels to
enter Noah's ark 69

Antediluvians
instructed by angels
directly from Christ
65

Ark of the covenant
always accompanied by
four angels 109
living angels stand at
both ends of in the
heavenly sanctuary
100

Blind persons
angels save from
manifold dangers 15

Cain
did not repent even
after an angel talked
with him 65

Christ
appeared as an angel to
Gideon 113
appeared as an angel to
Israel in the time of

regarding the building
of a temple 129

Demons
see *Evil angels*

Eden
remained on earth long
after sin, guarded by
angels 63

Elijah
fed by an angel morn-
ing and evening 130
surrounded on Mt.
Carmel by a host of
angels 130

Elisha
ministered to by angels
during his final illness
134

Enoch
borne to heaven in
flaming chariots 68
Ellen White saw in a
world with seven
moons 68
represents those
translated without
dying 68

Ethiopian eunuch
attended by angels 227

Eve
after eating the forbid-
den fruit felt like she
imagined the angels

felt 56
cautioned by angels not
to leave her husband's
side 52

Evil angels
acknowledge Christ's
deity at the end of
time 277
assume human form in
the last great conflict
261
assume the form of
dead friends in order
to deceive 124
complained bitterly
when Jesus was
resurrected 210
cannot destroy the
weakest of God's
saints 140
constantly seeking
access to God's people
12
controlled priests and
rulers at Jesus' trial
199
enshrouded Jesus on
the cross 203
exulted around Jesus'
tomb 204
feared Daniel's influ-
ence 141
lead people to believe
their dead loved ones
are angels 262
were among Christ's